Realism in American Fiction

REALISM IN AMERICAN FICTION

Contribution of William Dean Howells

Sangeeta Handa

Rawat Publications
Jaipur and New Delhi

ISBN 81-7033-650-3

Published by
Prem Rawat for ***Rawat Publications***
Satyam Apartments, Sector 3, Jain Temple Road,
Jawahar Nagar, Jaipur 302 004 India
Phone: 0141 651748 / 657006 Fax: 0141 651748
e-mail: rawatbooks@pinkline.net

Delhi Office
G-4, 4832/24, Ansari Road, Daryaganj, New Delhi 110 002
Phone: 3263290

Typeset by Rawat Computers, Jaipur
Printed at Nice Printing Press, New Delhi

Contents

Preface

This book attempts to study William Dean Howells' contribution as a pioneer in ushering in an era of American realism in the history of American literature.

Realism has been a subject of interest with critics of all times, although in the contemporary times it is mostly redundant and outdated. But can there exist any work of creation, without the lurking traces of realism? In fact, with the onset of modernist, post-modernist, post-post-modernist tendencies, the strong position of realism has been challenged.

In America, it was Howells who developed the literary theory of realism and extricated the American novel from the clutches of the sentimental novel. Howells' literary span, which covers almost half a century (1870-1920), is a monumental record of carefully constructed narrative ranging from plays, poems and critical essays to travelogues, fiction, editorial comments and sketches. The sheer volume and variety of his work—137 volumes of one sort and another, 35 novels and ceaseless critical comments, attests to his realistic creed. In fact, his work marks an immense resource of understanding of life in America during the last half of the nineteenth century, because as the Dean of American Letters he dominated the literary scene of America for almost three decades.

This text is a revised version of the doctoral thesis written under the supervision of late Dr. G.S. Rahi of Punjabi University, Patiala. I am indebted to him for his patient and sustained guidance in formulating my views. The American Studies Research Centre sanctioned a Teacher's Study Grant and made it possible for me to fully exploit the resources of the Centre. I owe a debt of gratitude to Dr. G.S. Sekhon who inspired me to revise the thesis. Last, but not the least, my thanks to my immediate family members who patiently cooperated with me in every possible way.

Sangeeta Handa

Introduction

William Dean Howells (1837-1920), a pioneer in American realism, is a neglected novelist in the history of American literature. Being an editor of the leading literary monthly for almost three decades, Howells was solely responsible for ushering in a new era in the art of novel writing. In fact, it was Howells who drew attention towards Henry James and Mark Twain and as a generous critic, recognized the signs of true genius in both of them and in many subtle ways guided their development too. But ironically, as a novelist, Howells' reputation is not only not at par with these writers, it is virtually obliterated in the current literary scene of America. John W. Crowley, in his introduction to *The Mask of Fiction: Essays on W.D.H.*, gives a brief account of Howells' dwindling reputation. He writes:

> When *The Critic* invited its readers, in 1884, to nominate 'Our Forty Immortals' for a hypothetical American Academy, Howells placed fifth behind Oliver Wendell Holmes...but well ahead of Henry James and S.L. Clemens (thirteenth and fourteenth respectively)... By 1951, however, when scholars were

> explaining *Eight American Authors: A Review of Research and Criticism* (1956), which may be regarded as the academic equivalent of the Academy, Howells was suggested for inclusion but rejected.[1]

Howells approached fiction tentatively, through criticism and travel-writing and from capturing the externalities of contemporary reality, he entered into the inner complexities of the human mind. The son of an Ohio country newspaperman, Howells spent his youth in small town newspaper offices, unconsciously assimilating the western egalitarianism, the knowledge of which he fully conveyed in his fiction. In fact, it was his great attachment to western egalitarian values that kept his vision of the west as an ideal land of freedom, equality and purity always alive. Later, when he came in contact with the city life of Boston and New York and felt the loss of these values, he could not fully reconcile to the new set of principles emerging in these urban centers. In many of his novels, especially the ones he wrote during his most mature phase as a writer, he has authentically captured this sense of irreconcilability. As Jay Martin comments: "Between Boston, Europe and Frontier Ohio; East and West, Culture and Anarchy, Society and Self, the lines of force were drawn."[2]

Even after getting into the circle of the New England Brahmins, like Lowel, Holmes and Hawthorne, Howells did not forsake his frontier roots and tried to cling to the democratic simplicity of western equable values. In quite a number of his novels, he took up the theme of the social contradictions in American society and tried to assert the superiority of the West, where he believed that people still possessed the sense of goodness, which was completely eroded in the East. For the evidence of the validity of his contention, Howells created innumerable situations in his fiction.

However, till the last moment of his life, Howells did not lose faith in the lingering goodness in man, though his fiction, as he grew in experience of life, showed signs of pessimism and cynicism to a much greater degree than his earlier fiction.

During the last decade of his life, his novels became indigestible for literary palates and he became a 'Dead Cult' in his own lifetime. It was Lewis' Nobel Prize speech, of course, that greatly affected Howells' literary reputation, though the derogatory comments of Atherton, H.L. Mencken, John Macy and Van Wyck Brooks had also done considerable harm to his reputation. For quite some time, the critical opinion remained influenced by the comments of these detractors.

However, during 1930s and 1940s, a few sympathetic readers, such as Walter Fuller Taylor and George Arms tried to evince some interest in Howells by focusing on the economic and social aspects of his novels. After the war, a sincere effort was undertaken by critics like Everett Carter to reclaim Howells' reputation. In his prologue to *Howells and the Age of Realism*, Carter gave Howells full credit for initiating the realistic movement in America. In the pioneering works of George Arms, Edwin H. Cady, James Woodress, William M. Gibson, George N. Bennett, Olov Fryckstedt, Rudolf and Clara Kirk and others, Howells' *The Realist* took shape. In most of these critical commentaries, the realism of Howells was analyzed from the point of view of his own comments about various influences in his life. That is to say, that much of criticism, as before, focused less on the art of fiction and more on its social implications.

The credit of bringing Howells to the modernist pedestal goes to Richard Foster, who, in his seminal essay 'Contemporaneity of William Dean Howells' brought to light certain features of Howells' art by which he can be considered as a modernist progenitor. He comments that his "works have as yet unrecognized depth and quality of insight into the predicaments of what we call 'the modern world'."[3] Whereas Carter offers fresh critical insights into Howells world by defending the intellectual and artistic integrity of his realism, Foster moves a step further by pointing at the richness and depth of Howells' art as a writer of great fiction. He has tried to locate his individuality outside the realistic creed, without robbing him of his historical incidence.

In the more recent assessments of Howells by the revisionist scholars like George C. Carrington Jr., Kenneth S. Lynn, John W. Crowley and Kermit Vanderbilt, a new image of Howells has been projected in which he has been shown to be a man racked by existential doubts and neurotic visitations. Carrington, in the analysis of Howells' novels has totally reversed the earlier view held by critics like Edwin Cady who believed that "the primary source of his inability was simply that life long psychological difficulties left Howells with a neurotic condition which literally made it impossible, for him to know and understand, as realities, the position of pain and filth and terror in human living with which a major writer must be at least vicariously intimate."[4]

John W. Crowley, in his recent book *Mask of Fiction*, has once again related the incomplete world of Howells to the presence of homosexual tendencies and some obscure hurt in his youth. Michael Davitt Bell, another recent critic also suggests that Howells' realism may be understood as a response to a gender anxiety induced by mid-nineteenth century encoding of the artist as 'effeminate'.[5]

Such scattered commentary on Howells' prudishness and restrictive Victorian sensibility cannot obscure the range of his extraordinarily sensitive sensibility. As Carrington shows, each of Howells' novel depicts his keen knowledge of the unsmiling aspect of life, which was supposed to be missing from his earlier work. He also suggests that the commonplace in Howells is "potent and sometimes threatening, and is at any rate, plentifully offset by violence, horror, blackness and the other gothic traits admired by present day critics."[6]

The present work attempts to establish Howells' contribution to the development of realistic theory in a wider perspective. Once again the deeper and profound strands of his work have been picked up, to show that working fully inside the norms of realistic theory, he could produce novels of moral and psychological significance. As he himself belonged to the middle class, the issues concerning the struggling middle-class milieu surface most in his works. In one of his novels *The Rise of Silas Lapham*, Tom Corey and Silas Lapham are on an excursion steamer, which is crowded with fun loving middle and lower class Americans and the author comments about these people that they "... looked as if they might not only be easily but safely known. There was little style and no distinction among them... In fact, they were commonplace, with nothing but the American poetry of vivid purpose to light them up, where they did not wholly lack fire."[7]

It is to these so-called commonplace people, without much style and distinction, that Howells' probing eye turns again and again and it is in their dull, prosaic, simple lives that he beautifully captures the "American poetry of vivid purpose". Initially, it was the idealization of human condition against which Howells chose to write, and in doing so, wrote novels with clear and explicit anti-romantic stance. Gradually, the force of his vehement anti-sentimental viewpoint gave way to the authenticity of lived experience, which expanded to the larger social and moral perspective.

A general argument is set out in Chapter 1, which is pursued throughout the thesis as a whole. Thus, while later chapters seek to illuminate specific novels of Howells, a connecting line of thought is also intended. In Chapter 1, realism is put in its broadest perspective by placing divergent definitions and views on realism together. The purpose is to acquaint the reader with the implications of this term and to specify the kind of realism with which Howells is concerned. In Chapter 2, a brief survey is made of the factors responsible for the rise of realism in world literature with special reference to America. The final argument that comes up after analyzing the reasons for the rise of realism in specific countries, is that, though in each country there were particular reasons for the growth of realism, yet, overall, the growth of this phenomenon was also related and acquired to some extent.

The central argument of this study will be worked out in the analysis of the major works of Howells. As has been pointed out, the body of Howells' writings is so large that it is virtually impossible to analyze it all. Otherwise also, apart from the novels discussed in this study, the rest of Howells' work is not so relevant to the realistic aspect with which the present study is mainly concerned. Thus, the main focus will be on his major works: *Their Wedding Journey, A Foregone Conclusion, A Chance Acquaintance, A Modern Instance, The Rise of Silas Lapham, Indian Summer, A Minister's Charge, The Landlord at Lion's Head*. While the nature of the argument does not exclude any specific work of Howells, this delimitation is dictated due to the necessity of clarity. In each chapter, a specific theme has been picked up and two or three of his major works have been analyzed under that theme. The themes which have been picked up for analysis are those which are most recurrent in Howells' novels. In the re-evaluation of the themes, the main focus is on

Howells' realistic creed and, in fact, all the novels have been discussed from the point of view of realism.

On reading Howells' realistic novels, an astute reader can discern certain themes and motifs which surface prominently in his fiction. One of these is the anti-romantic stance which Howells took in order to highlight the importance of realism. In Chapter 3, the reader is briefly acquainted with Howells' transition from an idealist to a realist. Howells, who initially admired the great romantic and idealist writers, gradually lost faith in such books, that in his view, provided the reader with a false view of life. In his first novel, *Their Wedding Journey*, Howells, in order to unleash the veil of unreality, wrote about the wedding journey of the newlyweds, Isabel and Basil March, the couple who later on appears in his novel *A Hazard of New Fortunes* too. These two novels written at totally different stages of Howells' career show the disenchantment, which the discovery of truth brings in one's life.

Though Howells declared his intention to cling to the smiling aspects of middle-class existence, yet, eventually, he found that in the affairs of the middle-class people, there were more unsmiling aspects which could not be ignored. The recognition of this fact became apparent for the first time in his major novel *A Modern Instance*, a detailed study of which has been taken up in Chapter 4. This novel clearly marks Howells' growth as a realist because in spite of being a poignant story of unhappy marriage ending in a separation, it does not end in a tragedy. In his realistic theory, Howells did not keep any place for tragedy, which he thought, was based on unrealistic and false notions. Another novel, *The Landlord at Lion's Head*, written at a much later phase of his literary career, shows the same kind of stark realism. In both the novels, Howells has tried his best not to give tragic conclusion, yet, the blatant reality of the situation, as projected in these novels, clearly conveys the sense of stark pessimism.

In Chapter 5, two novels, namely, *The Rise of Silas Lapham* and *The Minister's Charge* have been taken up. In both the novels, Howells takes up the popular success myths in order to give a realistic treatment to them. In the character of Silas Lapham, he shows a rich man who has acquired a lot of wealth by dint of hard work. Such characters fascinated the American psyche, but Howells in this novel, gives a realistic treatment to the aftermath of success with which people were mostly not familiar. The life of a successful man, as Howells shows in this novel, is not a pleasant story after all. In the moral rise and financial ruin of the protagonist, Howells shatters the image of the businessman, who could always manoeuvre and maintain wealth. In *The Minister's Charge*, once again Howells shows that the road to success, in spite of hard work, is not so smooth. In the format of the popular story paradigm, Howells presents the true picture of success and a successful man.

Instead of making attempts at imagining noble instances of human self-sacrifice, lofty aspirations and soul-stirring passion, Howellsian realism significantly highlighted the beauty in mediocrity and the commonplace. In Chapter 6, three novels, written in different phases of Howells' life, have been taken up in order to show the realistic treatment Howells gives to love. The novels taken up in this chapter are *A Foregone Conclusion, The Lady of the Aroostook* and *Indian Summer*. Romantic love is the prime subject matter of these three novels and in all the three the romantic illusion of the lovers is ultimately shattered. Howells' realistic sword, once again, cuts to pieces the romantic citadels of imaginary minds.

Chapter 7, which is the concluding part of this study, contains an assessment of the art of William Dean Howells and the relevance of realism in the present context. The reasons for the gradual decline of realism as a genre have been traced. An effort has been made to highlight all the factors, social, political and aesthetic responsible for total disappearance of realism. What emerges from the study is that though apparently realism appears to have been lost in the emerging scene of modernist and post-modernist writing, yet, it seems, that a time has come when the need for realistic writing is going to dominate the literary scene. Literature cannot thrive merely on sweet imaging and idealistic concoctions alone.

Howells has been praised to the skies by critics and scholars. He has also been condemned, criticized and discarded repeatedly by opinion makers. But he refuses to stay buried. Someone is forever rediscovering and attempting to redefine the vitality of art and ideas, the significance of his theory of realism and its practice in fiction. The history of his reputation is unique in American literature and a thorough study of it would be revealing as well as intriguing.

A highly versatile and prolific writer like Howells cannot be understood from the point of view of realism alone, yet the nature of study has put such arbitrary bindings that it has become necessary to limit the argument. A sincere effort has been made, to fully explore the fundamental issues with the help of diverse and opposite view points of critics and a new approach has been evolved.

Notes

1. John W. Crowley, *The Mask of Fiction; Essays on W.D.H.* (Amherst: University of Massachusetts Press, 1989): 3-4. The ups and downs of Howells' literary reputation, such as these, have been charted many times by various scholars and critics writing on Howells. But the fact remains that his influence as a critic and as a pioneer in realism remains till now. In fact, so great was his influence, that writers growing up in the early twentieth century, wrote with the specific purpose of dissociating themselves from Howellsian realism.
2. Jay Martin, *Harvests of Change: American Literature 1865-1914* (Englewood Cliffs: Prentice Hall, 1967): 38.
3. Richard Foster, "The Contemporaneity of Howells", *New England Quarterly*, 32 (1959): 54-55.
4. Edwin H. Cady, "The Neuroticism of William Dean Howells", *MLA* 61 (1946): 229.
5. Michael Davitt Bell, "The Sin of Art and the Problem of American Realism: William Dean Howells", *Prospects*, 9(1984): 116.
6. George C. Carrington, Jr., *The Immense Complex Drama: The World and Art of the Howells Novel* (Columbus: Ohio State University Press,1966): 18.
7. William Dean Howells, *The Rise of Silas Lapham* (New York: Rinehart, 1949): 84.

1

Realism: The Background

"Reality is like a float that rides all efforts of the irritated mind to frame its definition, or a fish that swallows up all other forms of life and then drinks off the sea in which it swims."[1] To say that realism is an enigma or a riddle is not far-fetched. Any attempt at its definition has almost always generated a distortion, because it is a pluralistic term, and cannot be reduced to a simple definition.

To trace the birth of realism from the vast realm of literature is as futile an urge, as an urge for the touch of the horizon, because the deeper we delve to cull out its origin, the more abstract it becomes. The reason is obvious. Realism is as old as literature itself because art and life are the two sides of the same coin and a writer's greatest source of creation is life, with its crude realities. So, in a rudimentary form, realism has always been present in all creative writing. Apart from the specific beginning of realism in the literatures of various countries, the presence of a realistic streak (even when it had not developed as a self-conscious genre) has been established. Becker has rightly pointed out that "...realism in literature has always existed, though... almost always in quantity or degree far short of what constitutes a literary movement or mode."[2]

Talking of the "fundamental epistemological problem of the relation of art to reality. René Wellek, in his treatise on realism, has tried to give a rounded relationship between art and reality, when he says: "Art cannot help dealing with reality, however much we narrow down its meaning or emphasize the transforming or creative power of the artists."[3]

After accepting that the streak of realism always lurked in the literary traditions of this world there are certain basic questions which are large and hence not easy to approach, but which need answers, even though they have been answered variously. Literature on realism is immense.[4] What was is that led to the rise of realism, approximately at the same time in the literature of the countries far and wide? What is the genesis of realism as a movement in world literature? What necessitated the rise of realism, particularly in the latter half of the nineteenth century? Was it something to do with the rising middle class? Was it a reaction to romantic satiety? Or was it the result of the declining moral values which required to be mirrored through realism? Borus' assessment is correct to a certain point when he says: "We know much of what realism was (and is), but we know less about why realism was."[5]

In spite of being an almost indispensable area of the world literature and an influential literary genre, realism due to its inherent fluidity and multifaceted perspective has been a very unstable term. Even if this semantic flux is left alone, it can generate a meaning in the critical context itself. René Wellek has excellently followed the 'sinuosity' of this term and has even specified how and when this term originated in painting and philosophy and how gradually it entered the area of literature.[6] In fact, prior to the established connotation which the term has acquired in the modern context, the history of realism as a term in literature, is quite vague. Before the term was coined for the first time by Champfleury's essay "Le Realism", realism had not acquired any specific meaning and was more or less equated with terms like 'materialism' or 'local color'.

Thus, we see that realism is a broad concept, and it has been interpreted so differently that it has no exclusive standpoint. In philosophy it has a kind of philosophical meaning, in sociology it can be interpreted in sociological terms and in literature it adopts a literary taint. Harold H. Kolb, Jr. also points at "the related fallacies of reification, in which the defined term takes on a life of its own, apart from the literature which nourishes it."[7] Even in various dictionaries it has different connotations. Seeing so much of elasticity and variation, Mark Kinkeadweek and Ian Gregor have made a very apt remark that "realism is a notoriously treacherous concept."[8]

The unpredictability of this involved term is also due to a highly blurred view of reality and its interrelation with art. There is a sharp dichotomy between the exterior world of practical, everyday, 'business in life' and the interior world of the artists, of the work of vision and the uses of imagination. In what does reality reside? Is it in things, practical action (social or political), in day-to-day life, in other people, other relations and dealings with them or in art and uses of imagination, in the life of the mind? Such questions, which harass the mind have been the matter of unsolved equation, for the literatti and writers and critics of all ages. Commenting on the fluctuating nature of reality, Lukacs comments: "Reality is neither static nor constant, the investigator cannot exhaust its substance. It is, on the contrary, a constant flux---only revealing a definite though never simple direction to the eye of the trained observer."[9]

The realistic priority of every writer remains different. What is realistic and real for one writer may not be so for the other. With some realists this priority lies in the depiction of the typical and the ordinary, thus projecting the blander aspects of middle class existence. With others, reality resides in the language of the mind and motives and with still others it lies in the social structure, in man and his environment. Anything entering the realm of art and literature is always real, but what emerges out of art and literature has to undergo a selective process and what finally emerges in this creative enterprise, is not reality but the semblance of reality, at is best. Viewed from this angle, as Pierre Machery shows, it appears as if reality and realism in literature are incomplete terms. "The enterprise of thought is inherently provisional, culminating in its own abolition when it is reassimilated into an unmodified, merely interpreted reality."[10]

So, like realism, the concept of reality remains like a ball in a writer's court, which he can kick anywhere according to his necessity and suitability. Reality, as such, assumes a very subjective colour due to its indeterminate character. Because of the shifting modes of reality, the definition of realism remains an incomplete affair and it adopts a different form with every philosopher, writer and critic and takes up a relativistic stance. Virginia Woolfe's remark is quite relevant here: "Reality is something very erratic, very undependable---now to be found in a dusty road, now in a scrap of newspaper in the street, now in a daffodil, now in a sun."[11]

The best of realistic art provides only an illusion of reality, not reality, which is an "alternative order which artificiality of art provides".[12] The greatness of a realistic writer lies in his ability to make us believe and get influenced by that illusion of reality, created by the artificiality of art. If we enter into this endless argument of what is real and what is reality in life, leave aside in art, even then it is most difficult to know a person fully. It is a fact that even in the closest of human relationships, we cannot fully claim to 'know' another person. Our assessment of the other person is based on "shaky inferences"[13] which we presume are perhaps real, but eventually, may not be real after all. The working of the human mind is a complex phenomenon and the identity of a real being is revealed to the person himself through "reliable internal signs"[14] and no one else. Even a writer of very accurate and penetrating observation, at the most, comes very close to reality, but never reaches it. In the production of art, reality is further removed, as it is accompanied by the process of imagination, which is the most important ingredient of a creative process. What then is realism in literature? It is a kind of "tacit assumption" which the reader is conditioned to share with the writer that "a human life is most truthfully presented in terms of the individual's milieu, of particularity of social situation and historical circumstance."[15]

Any literary work gets its place and type fixed on the basis of two important aspects---form and content. A writer writing under a realistic norm has to stick to certain codes of realistic convention as displayed through its narrative technique and content. In theory, there have been rigorous codes of realistic convention, yet in practice these codes have not been pursued diligently by the realists. Hence, none of the codes of realism are essential, though they may be very important. For example, transcription of facts is an important aspect to be dealt with by a realistic writer and that fact has to be and is generally based on observation and experience. But the observation is ultimately based on personal perception and the field of experience is obviously individual. This field of experience may encompass the common man, ordinary events (as in the case of William Dean Howells) or deal with exalted milieu (as in the case of Edith Wharton). Apart from the depiction of the external facets of experience which vary a lot from realist to realist, there is a strong desire to unfold the internal fact because whatever field of experience a realist may depict, it always borders on moral experience.

The best technique for solving internal-external equation for a realist has been in the use of dramatic method which ensures maximum objectivity and impersonality. More important than the mere assimilation of external fact is the power to authenticate the external-internal equation in convincing and plausible tones. A need to maintain balance between the perceiving and creative mind has been the most important requirement for a realist. He has to maintain a neutral stance and avoid all kinds of resolved conclusions. He has to clinch the issue (the choice of issue is not restricted, it can be social, economic, psychological or moral) though Becker points out that it is better for a realist to deal with "those elements in the objective world which strike all minds in much the same way."[16] A realist's task is to present the issue as it is, without moral pronouncements or authorial commentary or clear-cut solutions. Becker cites a few examples from the works of famous realists where the objectivity which he calls 'scrupulosity' is violated. In spite of their flawed narrative, from the point of view of realism, they have been recognized as best realists because even by violating the norm of objectivity they have successfully managed to authenticate the external-internal equation through the moral experience of their work. Thus, realism, as Becker remarks, ultimately remains a "bundle of tendencies" because " no areas are barred to a realist" as "reality is in the writer's vision rather than in the selection of this or that particular theme."[17]

To impose any kind of artlessness on the work of art can be the work of a very artful bent of mind. The work of a realist requires that self conscious artlessness which can give a natural hue and order to the otherwise "chaotic and raw reality". Emilé Zola, commenting on scientific realism says: "In fact, the whole operation consists in taking facts from nature, then in studying the mechanism of these facts, acting upon them, by the modification of circumstance and surroundings, without deviating from the laws of nature. Finally, you possess knowledge of him, in both his individual and social relations."[18]

But this vision of reality remains personal and subjective. In theory, the realists have been advocating the benefits of maintaining objectivity and giving top priority to the presentation of the objective truth, yet in practice they have not been able to maintain this standard and have realized the fundamental fallacy of the doctrine of objectivity. What a realist can do at best, as Kolb remarks, is to "strive for the illusion of objectivity".[19]

Realism is a doctrine, a concept and a discipline. It is a "semantic house of many mansions".[20] As a theory, it definitely has certain codes of artistic conventions. That is why, in René Wellek's view, it is ultimately "bad aesthetics".[21] As has been suggested by several critics and commentators, realism is another name for decadent deterministic humanism. So moralistic and didactic strain touching upon social problems has surfaced in the realistic writings of many realists, especially William Deal Howells, who is the topic of the present study. More often, realism as a literary theory with clearly defined postulates is not viewed as an artistic achievement and the followers of this convention, as William Dean Howells was, have been the target of disparaging comment. Robert Scholes discredits realism because it "exalts life and diminishes words".[22] It has been rejected by its detractors as a fallacy, an impossibility and a realist's work as the unreal world of fact. So, the confusion persists and controversy lingers on. As a heterogeneous movement, realism, cannot be reduced to a simple definition and any effort to the contrary, mars the depth and fecundity of this term, because certain extra-textual elements in the description of realism cannot simply be ignored.

Edwin H. Cady has tried to reach the definition of realism, in spite of its being a circular term. In the eventual analysis of this term, he has highlighted many misconceptions which exist in the understanding of realism and reality. His argument is based on the thesis that realism has nothing much to do with reality in the ordinary sense of the word, because reality in the social as well as psychological realm is a "flowing abstraction".[23] Literary realism is ultimately dependent upon a theory of common vision and the common vision, according to Cady, is what is generally referred to as 'reality'. Though realism has been dubbed as dull, boring and uninteresting and factual, yet it simply cannot be denied that it is very difficult to make rhetorical construction of reality. Reality cannot be taken for granted as it is a continuous process that never allows the word to offer a convenient mould of meaning. Actual reality tends to be subjective and the high water mark of realism is to achieve a kind of detached objectivity. Thus, there is a kind of inherent paradox in the term 'realism' itself which does not let it possess a stable viewpoint.

Alfred Habegger, in his analysis of realism, has tried to dissociate the definition of realism from the fixed opinions by the established critics. René Wellek's definition of realism as "description of contemporary social reality" in Habegger's view does not explain the larger corpus of realistic fiction which includes such divergent realists like Mark Twain, Henry James, William Dean Howells, H.H. Boyesen, Joseph Kirkland, Henry Adams, etc. For that matter, no single definition of realism fully envelops the 'realism' of all the realistic writers. The description of contemporary social reality is just one important aspect of realistic fiction, which a realist may or may not use in his novel. Wellek's definition of realism, which is based on 'period concept' does not explain realism in totality as it completely ignores the "dialectical nature of realism".[24] So we can fully endorse Habegger's view that "no art can be defined fully by referring to its subject-matter."[25] Even Lukacs, while making a distinction between critical realism and socialist realism, says, that in both, the question of perspective is very important and "this perspective will vary in form and content according to the level of social development and the subject matter".[26] The content of any realistic fiction should be theoretically authentic. For the content to be authentic, it is generally assumed that it should deal with the present, the contemporary and objective view of society. But again, many times, realists indulge in debunking factuality. Gordon Haight's definition of realism appears more objective and seem to encompass the features of realistic fiction to a larger extent, when he defines a realist's aim as "an accurate, objective reproduction of scene and character for its own sake."[27] Yet, this definition once again is incomplete, as it suggests that realism is not supposed to make any judgment on its material and subject-matter.

Complete absence of any kind of critical judgment and total detachment of the writer is not a prerequisite for a realistic writing and such notions have often been misleading and pose a hindrance in the understanding of realism. One is reminded of Wayne C. Booth's comment here, when he says: "We must never forget that though the author can, to some extent, choose his guises, he can never choose to disappear."[28] A mere heaping up of facts and accurate realistic details, do constitute an important aspect and technique of realism, yet a meaning has to emerge out of the work of art, whether the meaning is contained in the content, style or point of view, that is the author's choice.

In this matter of opinions, comments, generalizations and analyses, once again the real definition of realism is lost. In retrospect, one realizes the futility of arriving at a definition, when we know that no work of realistic art fully fits in any definition of realism. Realism, ultimately, remains a theory and when this theory is used in practice by a realist, however hard he may try, the two (theory and practice) do not overlap completely to present a unified whole. That perhaps is an impossibility and if at all any writer (so far no author has achieved this feat) is successful in presenting a unified whole of the theory and practice of realism in fiction, that would only result in a documentary, or a dull replica of life, without any meaning and attraction. To sum up the discussion on realism, one may rest content with the remark that Berthoff Warner gives about literary history, that it is an "impossible genre".[29]

Notes

1. As quoted in Damian Grant, *Realism* (London: Methuen, 1970):8.
2. George J. Becker, *Realism in Modern Literature* (New York: Ungar, 1980).
3. René Wellek, "The Concept of Realism in Literary Scholarship", *Concepts of Criticism* (London: New Haven, 1963): 224.

4. The following books are only a sample of the works on the genre: Berthoff, *The Ferment of Realism*; Brooks, *The Confident Years*; Cady, *The Light of Common Day*; Chase, *The American Novel and its Tradition*; Kazin, *On Native Grounds*; Kolb, *The Illusion of Life*; Martin, *Harvests of Change*; Michaels, *The Gold Standard and the Logic of Naturalism*; Parrington, *The Beginnings of Critical Realism*; Pizer, *Realism and Naturalism*; Sundquist, *American Literary Realism*; and Trachtenberg, *The Incorporation of America.*

   The major realistic tracts include: Dreiser, "True Art Speaks Plainly", Howells, *Criticism and Fiction*; Howells, *Literature and Life*; Garland, *Crumbling Idols: Twelve Essays on Art and Literature*; James, *The Art of Fiction*; James, *The Future of the Novel*; James, *Partial Portraits*; James, *Notes on Novelists*; Norris, *The Responsibilities of the Novelists*; and Twain, "Fenimore Cooper's Literary Offenses."

5. Daniel Borus, *Writing Realism: Howells, James and Norris in the Mass Market* (Chapel Hill: University of North Carolina Press, 1989): 1.

6. Wellek, 228.

7. Harold H. Kolb Jr. *The Illusion of Life: American Realism as a Literary Form*. (Charlottesville: University Press of Virginia, 1969): 11.

8. Mark Kinkeadweek and Ian Gregor quoted by Grant 2.

9. Georg Lukacs, *The Meaning of Contemporary Realism*, trans. John and Necke Mander (London: Merlin Press, 1964): 67.

10. Pierre Machery, *A Theory of Literary Production*, trans. Geoffery Wall (London: Routledge and Kegan Paul, 1978): 6.

11. Virginia Woolfe, *A Room of One's Own* (New York: Harcourt, 1957): 14.

12. D.A. Williams, ed., *The Monster in the Mirror: Studies in Nineteenth Century Realism* (Oxford: Oxford University Press, 1978): 5.

13. Wayne C. Booth, *The Rhetoric of Fiction* (Chicago: The University of Chicago Press, 1961): 3.

14. Booth, 3.
15. Williams, 6.
16. Becker *Realism*: 61.
17. Becker *Realism*: 48-49.
18. Emilé Zola, Qtd by Miriam Allot *Novelists on the Novel* (London: Routledge and Kegan Paul, 1980): 69.
19. Kolb, 34.
20. Grant C. Knight, *The Critical Period in American Literature*, (Chapel Hill: University of North Carolina Press, 1951): 73.
21. Wellek, 225.
22. Robert Scholes, *The Fabulators* (London: Oxford University Press, 1967): 35.
23. Edwin H. Cady, *The Light of Common Day. Realism in American Fiction* (Bloomington: Indiana University Press, 1971): 16, 19.
24. Alfred Habegger, *Gender, Fantasy and Realism in American Literature* (New York: Columbia University Press, 1982): 106.
25. Habegger, 106.
26. Lukacs, *Meaning*: 93.
27. Gordon S. Haight, "Realism Defined: William Dean Howells" Literary History of the United States ed., Robert E. Spiller and Others (New York: Macmillan, 1948, 11): 878.
28. Booth, 20.
29. Warner Berthoff, *The Ferment of Realism: American Literature 1884-1919* (New York: Free Press, 1965): 15.

2

Realism in World Literature

American realism at the turn of the century was not a mere local reaction to the series of developments in the post-Civil War America. It was a part of world movement---a movement which was readjustment to the new changes taking place in the field of industry, science, literature and art. There were many things happening at the same time the world over. There was a radical shift not only in industry, technology and science, but also in thoughts, perspectives and values. This age (1865-1914) was, as Jay Martin says, "a time particularly rich with relatedness—assumed, felt and actual---among people, ideas, convictions and the institutions of society."[1] It was a time of social change after much chaos of wars and revolutions, both religious and industrial. Out of the ruins of aristocracy, democracy had emerged, phoenix-like and with the birth of democracy and the spirit of nationalism, there was a rise of middle class. This sea-change had affected almost all the major countries of Europe, such as England, France, Unified

Germany, Italy and Russia, and its effect on the American scene was a natural corollary, this change being a contagious phenomenon. The change in the European worldview was not due to any single factor but due to the emergence of related factors, which, as chance would have it, happened at the same time. With scientific discoveries, the belief in the transcendental values and speculative idealism gave way to materialistic or atheistic philosophy. Growth of scientific culture definitely had such an impact on the writers the world over, that they simply could not bring themselves to writing unrealistic tales which merely provided aesthetic pleasure to the reading public ignorant of the developments of science. Writers as well as readers, both had become widely aware of the importance of factual evidence, which became the basic requirement of all literatures.

It was in France that the word 'realism' was used for the first time to define a literary method that attempted sincere and truthful imitations of the originals found in nature and its most important exponent in France was Balzac, who developed this genre in his *Comedie Humaine*. Balzac initiated interest in a realistic approach to literature by his inventive realism. He evinced interest in those aspects of life which had hitherto not been the subject of attention for writers. He was the precursor, and not a conscious realist nor a pioneer in the technical sense, as he did not formulate and set any rules for realistic convention.

Courbet's art struck a note in Champfleury's mind about the novelty of realism in painting and coincided with his photographic memory which he could effectively use in his fiction as he said, "what I see enters my head, descends through my arm and becomes what I have seen."[2] Balzac also got initiated into the realistic idea of treating humble peasants through a painting, yet he did not think in terms of realism and did not insist on purely mimetic urge. Rather he showed interest in the social problems and wrote to describe how people lived and how they behaved and how the social and economic factors controlled their way of living. Balzac was a trend-setter in originating the idea that man and his milieu are inseparable which later on became a fundamental postulate in socialist realism. Balzac's allegiance to unconscious realism provided enough ground for self-styled realists like Murger, Monnier and Duranty to codify and propagate a norm, which had characteristics of Balzac's realism.

Flaubert, who is regarded as the "father of realism", was in truth, vehemently opposed to realistic fiction, as he was of the firm opinion that art and reality are separate things. He believed in the aesthetic dimension of literature and could not reconcile to the opposing claims of art and reality. He did not believe in mirroring of reality as the object of true art. On the contrary, he insisted on the general and universal aspect of reality which he believed could be acquired through inferences and deductions made on the repeated patterns of human experience. In spite of his declared hatred for realism, his *Madame Bovary* is regarded as a masterpiece of realism. In this novel, Flaubert attempted a realistic portrayal of an emancipated woman contrary to the traditional figure with which the women in France were usually associated. The subject of the story in this novel was not new, as the feminist novels of this period was already dealing with the same storyline of a married woman having extramarital relationship with other men. But it was only Flaubert who did not try to redeem Madame Bovary of the sinful act of having adulterous relationships with men. Flaubert shows her as a self-centered young woman, who is dissatisfied with her husband due to insignificant failings in his character. From a commonplace domestic drama, Flaubert created a true picture of society of his times, because Madame Bovary's character is representative of many such frustrated women of those times whom nobody had dared to expose in writing yet.

The rise of the realistic novel in France and also in other parts of the world where it germinated is partly attributable to the rise of the middle class. But, in England the aristocratic class had not vanished as rapidly as the middle class had risen. So the realistic novel in England did not assume as sudden a sway as it did in America, France and Russia. The trend of realistic writing in England had tentative beginnings with the writings of Defoe and Fielding. The presentation of characters from the lower strata of society, like *Robinson Crusoe* and *Pamela*, was not received in a healthy spirit by the reading public of England. Except for these characters being from an ordinary middle class, there was nothing very realistic in the novels of these writers in the technical sense of the term. But to dare to come to the problems of the middle class in itself was an act of innovation and if Fielding and Richardson were not the realists, they were definitely pathfinders for the realist tradition, which was yet to begin. Their preliminary experiments in epistolary and memoir novel set the ball of realism rolling. Though the aims of these writers were to get at truth and authenticity, yet the technique used to authenticate their point was not well developed. In the case of Robinson Crusoe's struggle for prosperity through the exploitation of the meagre resources available, a parable of the middle-class struggle is written, yet the setting, which is a remote, uninhabited imaginary land, where Crusoe realizes his dreams, is most unrealistic.

The role of historical circumstances in the emergence of realism cannot be overlooked in the literature of any country, but in Russian literature, the role of historical circumstances in the emergence of realism was most dominant. Realism took deeper roots in Russian psyche, because due to its geographical setting it had never been much under the influence of the Renaissance. About this predisposition of the Russian psyche for factuality, R.H. Freeborn remarks: "Russian literature, when not obviously imitative, has tended to rejoice in factuality and the finiteness of experience in a way which always suggests that Russian sensibilities are happiest when located, fixed or rooted..."[3]

The 1840s were a time of important changes in Russian literature. Interest in the social environment, in the hidden motives of people's behavior, and in the laws and norms of community life became manifest. There was a great change in the conventional pattern of literary characters. Turgenev was the first one who felt the need for this change, because of the significant impact of westernism on him. Though he himself belonged to a wealthy background, he felt the need for greater participation of the middle class and lower middle class characters in the fictive scene of Russian literature. It was with his sincere efforts that clerks, craftsmen, actors, merchants and serfs burst into the foreground to share the stage with the higher classes. Turgenev strictly adhered to presenting an accurate description of contemporary peasants, totally eliminating anything heroic or melodramatic in his fiction. The topography and geography changed too as the scene shifted from claustrophobic drawing rooms to the "humdrum prosiness of life, seemingly devoid of any artistic interest."[4] Due to his education in Berlin and his closer association with Belinsky, Turgenev was greatly influenced by westernism, which aroused in him a strong desire for striving for the truth. Referring to the principles of his work, Turgenev once said: "To achieve a reproduction of the truth, the reality of life accurately and powerfully is the greatest happiness for a writer, even if this truth does not coincide with his own sympathies."[5] In his novels Turgenev described ordinary people who are typical of their times and social class. Committed to providing accurate pictures of contemporary life based on facts, he was sometimes accused of lacking the creative impulse, which is supposed to be the hallmark of great art. But, the difference in Turgenev's realistic vision as compared to the earlier Russian realists was noticeable. Though he did not enter into the psychological recesses of his characters' inner world the way Dostoyevsky and Tolstoy did, yet his intimate knowledge of his characters' mind, especially in depiction of the new social types in Rudin, Insarov and Bazarov made him a realist, who was a step ahead of the earlier Russian realists. This aspect of Turgenev had a most powerful impact on Howells, who remained his follower throughout his literary career. Even after the acknowledged influence of Tolstoy, Howells did not become the follower of his creative art as he did of Turgenev. He revered Tolstoy's moral world but he found that it did not coincide with his own realistic vision. Turgenev's dramatic method, with negligible intrusion of the author and utter fidelity to the truth remained for Howells a great treasure, as he confesses in *My Literary Passions*. "As for the people of his fiction, though they were of orders and civilizations so remote from my experience, they were of the eternal human types in whose origin and potentialities every one may find his heart, and I felt their verity in every touch."[6]

Tolstoy's and Dostoyevsky's contribution to the conventions of Russian realism related to ethical and social considerations rather than mere presentation of objective reality. For them, realism meant more than the copying of reality, it became more of a religious experience. Apart from offering the picture of contemporary society they no longer remained content with being mere chroniclers of their times. The moral thrust of their writing gave a new twist to the realism in their hands, as it assumed a psychological taint and became more of the realism of the mind. The presence of didactic intent, though unobstrusive, did not let these writers remain silent spectators of the human drama which they presented in their novels. They did not indulge in over-preaching, yet they always remained conscious of the good and bad, and in doing so, imposed a kind of moral order on the image of the world which they created in their fiction and made the reader acutely aware of that moral order. Talking of Tolstoy's moral code, Howells says: "Tolstoy tells us simply to live as Chirst bade us.... There's no more of it but Heaven knows that's enough, and hard enough."[7]

Tolstoy's realism bordered around the spiritual as well as social emancipation as he believed that there could be no moral justification for wealth amid mass poverty. Breaking with the aristocratic class Tolstoy went over to the side of the common people, whom he considered as the real makers of life. In his novels, he gave expression to his view of the deep crisis of Russian social order in the second half of the nineteenth century and brought to limelight the hardships associated with the peasant life. At first Howells was greatly influenced by Tolstoy's philosophy. But, in the flush of Tolstoyan enthusiasm, the novels he wrote showed more of his divergence from Tolstoy, because, he felt that Tolstoy's kind of realism was suited more to the Russian soil, than the American, as in America the social gap could not be bridged. This he shows in one of his later social novels *Annie Kilburn*.

Howells regarded Tolstoy as the supreme realist. Tolstoy's moral perspective on the subject of romantic and sexual love as depicted in *Anna Karenina* well suited Howells' perspective on romantic passion, the pursuance of which Howells considered as harmful which he showed in his novel, *A Modern Instance*. This quality of Dostoyevsky's realism was a step further in its totality and comprehensive perspective from Tolstoy in the sense that he did not append reality, but validated it by doubt like all truth. He did not engage his creative powers in presenting merely the contemporary reality, rather his keen and penetrating impulse could sense the illusory nature of reality. Although Tolstoy and Dostoyevsky continued the great realistic traditions of Fielding and Defoe, Balzac and Stendhal, yet the significant contribution of their kind of realism lies in the fact that they adhered to this creed when it was on the decline. In the case of Tolstoy, the principles he followed in his kind of realism objectively represent a continuation of the great realist school, yet subjectively, they grew out of the problems of his own time.

In America realism was much more than merely a borrowed label or a natural consequence of the fast spreading European realism. Even before the ground-breaking work of Howells in this field, the desire to capture the special immediate air of American reality in the familiar American dialect was quite apparent in Whitman's poetry. A new pattern of American literary history emerged, in which writers like Thoreau, Melville and Hawthorne were re-evaluated and a more sympathetic recognition was accorded to writers who were faithful to their materials and reflected the ideals and moods of their times. In this sense local colour was a precursor to realism. Most commonly, realism in America has been viewed as a movement in revolt against the literary trends prevailing in the mid-nineteenth century. Prior to Howells' self-conscious movement of realism, literary realism in American fiction was more or less concerned with rejection of the world of romance presented in the works of writers like Melville, Poe and Hawthrone.

There is no doubt that the character of American realism was forged due to the impact of Europe but that is not the whole story either. Opened to new varieties of experience,

American man was a changed man. In the post-Civil War world, man lost hold of the traditional values connected with the rural innocence of American mind. After the Civil War, there arose a sudden desire to search for the meaning of American identity and the true American spirit. In this effort for finding a national democratic character of America, the meaning of the new novel was evolved, which was surely going to be the realistic novel. De Forest, in his attempt to harmonize the dialectical contrariness associated with war, depicted the realistic battle scenes in his *Miss Revenel's Conversion* and thus initiated the awareness for realism in America. Thus, the changing spirit of American society called for a new materiality in fiction and the conditions of American life and culture were most ripe to receive this new materiality in the genre of realism. After the Civil War, realism in America became an essential literary means for coming to terms with the new American history---which included massive urbanization and the new democratic skepticism. In the age of pragmatism and social Darwinism, realism offered writers a redirection to explore the social facts.

Finally, the point that emerges very clearly from the definition of realism and its sudden emergence as a global phenomenon is that the conditions were most conducive for it in the late nineteenth century. The comparative review of European literature proves one more point that it was in France, that the interest in realistic subjects was initiated, but in other countries like England, Russia and America, interest in the realistic genre was also sprouting. The latter half of the nineteenth century in itself called for the rise in realism and a sudden emergence of middle class, growth of scientific temper and a desire for departure from romantic impulse were merely contributory factors which necessitated this change.

Notes

1. Jay Martin, Preface, *Harvests of Change: American Literature 1865-1914* (Englewood Cliffs: Prentice Hall, 1967).
2. Williams, 76.
3. Hemmings, F.W.J., 70.
4. Ivan Turgenev *Fathers and Sons: A Nest of Gentry: Novels*, trans. Bernard Issacs (Progress Publishers: Moscow, 1974): 8.
5. Ivan Turgenev, 7.
6. William Dean Howells, *My Literary Passions* (New York: Harper, 1910): 231-32.
7. As quoted in Louis J. Budd, "William Dean Howells' Debt to Tolstoy", *American Slavic and East European Review* 9 (1950): 295.

3

The Disenchanted Wings of Truth

"Who actually reads Howells' novel? Who even remembers their names."[1] This kind of critical opinion about Howells has put off many avid readers and researchers. Howells is one of those writers against whom such disparaging criticism has been very acute.[2] No writer for that matter, escapes negative criticism, but Howells is among those unlucky ones on whom the detractors have indulged in a lot of mud-slinging. Much of the derogatory criticism about Howells' achievement was also perhaps because he wrote and wrote and over-wrote. His prolificity got on people's nerves and the over-production of words was not to his everlasting credit. Howells dominated the literary scene of America at the end of the nineteenth century and beginning of the twentieth century due to his being associated with *Atlantic and Harpers* for quite some time. Apart from being a novelist, Howells dominated the literary scene as a critic too, making statements and forming critical opinion about the leading writers of the day. Being thoroughly conversant with eastern and western limits of America, Howells' fictive world is kaleidoscopic. As John Updike comments: "We are conscious of the wide spaces, psychological and even geographical..."[3] Jerry Herron very aptly calls him "serviceable Howells"[4] and observes that he provided an authority under whose aegis the disparate productions of American literary realism could function, both critically and fictionally.

What exactly a great novel is or should be is a moot point argued differently by various writers and critics. Judging from Wayne C. Booth's *The Rhetoric of Fiction* in which he has arbitrarily isolated technique from all the social and psychological forces that affect authors and readers, Howells' fiction does not lack anything in technique. "True novels must be realistic" argues Booth, for which the "center of consciousness has to work."[5] It requires a cautious temper not to step beyond the confines of probability while creating a work of fiction. Novel writing is not a spontaneous flow of powerful emotions as in the case of poetry and we do not have any poetic license in case of writing a novel. Recent commentators on the novel like Ian Watt and Arnold Kettle have discussed in detail how a novel should not just impose an idealist moral code and should rather aspire for what is true, so that the veil of unreality, the blurred vision is rendered correct. It is very true that the veil uncovered is much less stimulating invention and it does not give us the thrill of quickened fantasy, and perhaps this is what has happened with Howells, whose aim and purpose of writing throughout had been an all out effort to present before us the true picture, the real, the painful and plain, the simple and ordinary, which could not thrill.

Howells considered history, biography and autobiography much more authentic, and during the transitional period when sentimental and romantic era was on decline and realism had not held complete sway (as it did during the last decades of nineteenth century), there was a proliferation of autobiographies in literary field in America. In Howells' paradigm of realistic fiction, much was against the aesthetics of romance, idealism and sentimental fiction. He displayed an antipathy to all those writers whom he thought to be melodramatic, because he believed that it was in exalted fiction that falsity and untruth germinated and hence it posed a sort of threat to society. In his criticism too he fought a relentless war against sentimental and romantic fiction. In many of his reviews and critical comments Howells condemned writers like Hawthorne, Whitman, Dickens and Thackeray for painting an idealistic picture of life which, he thought was untrue.

The conflict and argument on the nature, genesis and craft of fiction goes on and the opinions as to what exactly a great novel should be, differ. Howells' novels have never been placed on a high pedestal and have failed, with the exception of a few works, to achieve the status of major classics. Even Howells' *The Rise of Silas Lapham*, his most famous and popular novel has never had an enthusiastic readership. Then, where does he fall short in achieving those heights, in spite of being a pioneer in the realistic genre, the great literary figure solely responsible for heralding a new movement in American fiction?

Howells claims in *Criticism and Fiction* that realism must 'map' life instead of picturing it and that "the artist lets us see the idea that resides in life."[6] Howells doctrine of writing insisted on the authenticity and "faithful treatment of material". But by this authenticity he did not mean the accuracy, which would just heap the facts. Instead he insisted that the artist's duty was to interpret human nature and to seek the universal in the individual rather than social interests.

Howells' limitations as a writer were many as he had to

scrupulously stick to his own convention of realistic writing and avoid the beaten track of sentimental practice and keep the melodramatic features completely out of his fictional world such as hyperbolic language, the idealistic scenes and sensational and tragic episodes. In fact, sometimes he has been accused of overindulging in the idealization of the commonplace. During the prenatal phase of the development of the realistic methods, Howells strove sincerely to reach the ideal which he had chalked out for realistic fiction. Even in his early fumbling as a writer of fiction his 'road to realism' never changed and his tract remained the same. But where he fails, as the common criticism against him is, that his conception of realism was highly individualized. Howells' earnestness and fidelity to truth was a special impulse and as an accomplished and conscientious writer he did not digress from the doctrine which he had undertaken to preach in literature. We miss a lot in his work, but we do not miss the truth.

From the production of words, in his father's Ohio Shop, to the literary setting of words as the editor of *Atlantic and Harpers*, the development of Howells' mind seems an easy journey, but on the contrary, it was a very complex process. Howells, who was initially expert at dealing with language as a commodity, as compositor, ultimately could not snap the tie successfully, when he entered into the literary world as a novelist. May be that is the reason why his novels sometimes have a journalistic flavor. Writing about his first attempt at fiction *The Independent Candidate: A Story of Today*, Howells confesses that he:

> composed the novel as he composed his other jobs and he stood at the type-case and assembled the words as they came to him. After the first few installments he discovered that he had absolutely no idea what to do with the story. His concern was, literally with

production: he had not foreseen the more elaborate economy of authorship.[7]

Why and when and how Howells became a realist cannot be traced and ascertained exactly, though it is very evident from his biographies and autobiographies that Howells was not a realist initially but an idealist as he himself confess in *My Literary Passions*, about the influence of Hawthorne on him. "He was always dealing with the problem of evil too, and I found a more potent charm in his more artistic handling of it than I found in George Eliot."[8]

The process of transition from an idealist and a romancer was not sudden, rather it was a slow process and it took Howells some years to finally become a hardcore realist. So much has been written on this particular aspect by Howells himself in his biographies that the argument cannot be stretched beyond this point. Family compulsions and financial burden kept him away from his 'literary intentions' temporarily, but it could not deter him for long to plunge into his vast accumulated resource of fiction, as he confessed to his friend M.M. Hurd. "I've got all other work off my hands and am pleasing myself with idea of romance. Everybody writes a novel sooner or later, and I expect it also in my destiny."[9] Before entering into the arena of the novel, he wrote a few travelogues like *Suburban Sketches* and *Venetian Life* which as Kenneth E. Eble declares, "are a highly successful fusion of Howells' literary and journalistic talents."[10] The novels which appear before the publication of *A Modern Instance* seem collectively to form an initial chapter in the growth and development of Howells' realism.

The usual categorization of Howells' novels has been based on the chronology of his novels. His novels have been critically examined on the basis of his early phase, when he stepped into the arena of fiction with half-set realistic postulates in his mind, tentatively exploring the idea of setting up his realistic terminology in the field of novel-writing. It has been the general critical opinion that the last decade of the nineteenth century forms the best and most mature phase of Howells, when he was fully in the grasp of his theory, which bordered around the ethical and social aspects of American life. In his writings of this phase, Howells tried to provide practical situations to the social as well as ethical problems of society. This practical approach towards the problems of suffering humanity and real interest in the minuteness of the experience of life is perhaps the basic feature of American realism, different in this aspect, from European realism. About this difference between American and European realism Alfred Kazin also comments:

> Realism in Europe found its philosophy in mechanism, its cosmogony in Newtonian conception of the universe, its authority in Comte, Darwin Taine... Realism in America, whatever it owed to contemporary skepticism and the influence of Darwinism, poured sullenly out of agrarian bitterness, the class hatred of the eighties and nineties, the bleakness of small-town life, the mockery of his *nouveaux riches*, and the bitterness of the great new proletarian cities.[11]

The later novels of Howells have received very less critical attention as they have been considered to be lacking in that profundity of thought which marked his mature phase. During the last phase, Howells' grip on realism loosened. Also, the rising tide of modernism and changed ideology gradually made Howells' realism inconsequent.

Howells' earlier work has been accused of lacking that comprehensive vision which marks his works of the mature phase. But on close analysis, it can be observed that traces of that profound moral and critical sense lurked in his earlier novels too, though it is not coherent to form a unified piece of perfect realistic art. His strong fidelity to truth and his obsession with realism is as strong in the beginning as it is in his later fiction.

A mere descriptive prose, *Venetian Life* established Howells' talent as a realistic writer. In this book, Howells openly stripped Venice of all the romantic illusions with which it was chiefly associated and highlighted the hidden decay crawling and gnawing the city mostly associated with beauty.

So, from the beginning we wee that Howells' intentions were clear. He was fully armed to blow the bubble of illusions and delusions. With his realistic writing he actually equipped himself to lay bare the hard realities of suffering humanity. He showed from the very beginning of his literary career that he possessed a force which would not let the common, simple and petty problems assume elevated and exaggerated heights and dwindle into tragedy. In his early novels, we get a glimpse of detached exploration of topics which did not have much of social and psychological overtones but it did have a moral strain. Of course, a sad sarcasm prevails, but it is not as piercing as in his later fiction. But in the earlier fiction Howells consciously worked out his variety of realism by a deliberate severance from whatever came under the head 'romance' or 'romanticism' and specially concentrated on the contemporary American scene. Habegger pinpoints this quality of Howells' realism which was so different from Henry James' variety of realism, when he says, "unlike James who worked out his variety of realism by recombining aspects of the tradition of the novel, Howells began by picking through the ashes and diamonds of American scene."[12]

Howells declared in the beginning of his literary career that he was interested in the insipid face of reality and knew very well that reality has an insipid face which may not be very popular with the reading public. His first book-length work of fiction *Their Wedding Journey*, which merely appears to be an idyll of delightful honeymooners, is a travelogue recording the happy journey of Basil and Isabel March from Boston to Niagra via New York, with return by way of Canada. In its early response, even by so discerning a critic like Henry James, the early writings of Howells seemed to lack "grasping imagination".[13] They gave a general impression of being merely technical exercises by which Howells got conversant with the art of novel-writing. That *Their Wedding Journey*, technically speaking, is not a perfect novel, is obvious. It has not a proper plot and apart from Basil and Isabel, it has no third character to be the focus of attention. Yet, in its limitations lay its positive features and as Bennett says, he gave "unity to the whole through the formal structure of the journey and through the personalities of the Marches."[14] Superficial study of the novel only shows it to be lacking in intensity, as Fryckstedt remarks: "His adherence to the commonplace solemnly proclaimed in *Their Wedding Journey* was no doubt seriously meant, but was hardly supported by any deeper vision of life."[15] It has merely been recognized as a fictional presentation of ordinary fact. The main thrust of Howells' realism was to narrow the gap between man and reality, and even in his earliest fiction this narrowing of the gap between man and reality remained of prime importance to him. In *Their Wedding Journey*, he rather inartistically talks of his literary intentions and mentally prepares his readers for the kind of fiction he is going to produce. His method, no doubt, is not fully mature, but his approach is definitely realistic. In *Their Wedding Journey* he declares his intention in a rather simple way when he says:

> As in literature the true artist will shun the use of real events if they are in improbable character, so the sincere observer of man will not desire to look upon his occasional phases, but will seek him in his habitual moods of vacancy and tiresomeness. To me, at any rate, he is at such times very precious, and I never perceive him to be so much a man and a brother as when I feel the pressure of his vast, natural, unaffected dullness, then I am able to enter confidently into his life and inhabit there, to think his shallow and feeble thoughts to be moved by his dumb, stupid desires, to be dimly illumined by his stinted inspirations, to share his foolish prejudices, to practice his obtuse selfishness. Yes, it is a very amusing world, if you do not refuse to be assumed...[16]

That the world of Howells' novels is going to be full of "vast, natural, unaffected dullness", "shallow and feeble thoughts", "dumb, stupid desires", "stinted aspirations" and "foolish prejudice" has led to the highly misplaced conception that Howells himself is dull and boring. It is in these "habitual moods of vacancy and tiresomeness" that the meaning of his realism resides. Those who expect something more than a mere commonplace and ordinary and hence find dullness and boredom in his fiction are targets of his satire. As Carrington observes, through his fiction, he is "satirizing the reader's expectations."[17]

Their Wedding Journey is no romantic love story and the title is ironic. It is no doubt a wedding journey of the newlyweds, but not a very young couple as both Basil and Isabel have delayed their marriage (Basil is thirty and Isabel is twenty-seven). They have reunited after a separation of eight years and the reason for their broken engagement is not specified. The novel launches Howells' anti-romantic ideology on an open note and explicit declaration when he doubts his "fitness for a sustained or involved narration, though I (he) am persuaded that a skillful romance could turn the courtship of

Basil and Isabel March to excellent account"(*Journey*: 1). He even makes his intention of sticking to "ordinary traits of American life" (p. 2) very clear. The use of travel structure in his early fiction, especially *Their Wedding Journey* served Howells' purpose of exposition of the variety of American people, their dispositions and their petty concerns, very effectively. In this book, there is a famous passage on 'realism', which has been largely interpreted and commented upon. "Ah ! Poor Real Life, which I love, can I make others share the delight I find in thy foolish and insipid face" (p. 67). The skeptical feeling, whether Howells will be able to make others share the delight in his realism is quite apparent in these lines.

In the recent critical analysis of the novel, much has been traced in this so-called just a wedding journey of the newlyweds. Allen F. Stein observes that it is the germination of the theme of marriage, which was to recur again and again in his novels to come that this novel serves as a prototype. In the marriage of honeymooning Marches, Howells shows a "key means of mitigating the threat of the confusion that lurks both in the external world and within oneself."[18] Even the illusion of the lack of pain, squalor and hard realities in Howells' fiction has been completely shattered by Cumpiano who has traced the presence of all this in *Their Wedding Journey*. Of course, the somber vision is more apparent in his later fiction, especially the fiction written during the last decade of the nineteenth century, yet the terror of the mysterious, violent, alien and often cruel has been detected in *Their Wedding Journey* too. Behind the facade of delicate irony and sprightly good humor there is "the terrifying potential below the surface of sunny, smiling American existence."[19] The honeymoon journey is beset with perils and hazards supposed to be missing during such trips. The couple see and feel the misery of many. Instead of the beautiful weather, they face stifling heat and contrary to the smooth journey, they face hazardous and risky ventures. The journey then, as Bassett suggests, becomes "an active metaphor---a renaming of America as they move simultaneously into past and future, origins and frontiers."[20]

Their Wedding Journey has also been considered as a search for the fictional method. "Leaving out fantasy, he tried to navigate between experience and conventional literary forms (romance), which throughout *Their Wedding Journey* suggest fiction-making or meaning devices necessary to the mediation of experience into fiction."[21] John K. Reeves, William M. Gibson and David L. Frazier have discussed this aspect of *Their Wedding Journey*.[22] Thus, *Their Wedding Journey* has a specific purpose to perform as it indicates a trend which his fiction was to follow later on. Its movement is a kind of "evolution into realism."[23]

This "evolution into realism" finds full force and expression in Howells' *A Hazard of New Fortunes*, in which Basil and Isabel March, the fictional couple appear once again as main characters. Apart from the re-appearance of the main characters Isabel and Basil, nothing much has been found in common in these two novels, as *Their Wedding Journey* is just the tentative fictional venture, whereas *A Hazard of New Fortunes* is the acme of Howells' literary career. Yet, on closer look, *A Hazard of New Fortunes* seems to form a sequel to *Their Wedding Journey*. It cannot be denied that it was written during the critical decade (last decade of the nineteenth century) when the growing agitation for reform was at its peak, and the impact of social and economic crisis on Howells' literary ideology was great. From the beginning of his literary career as a novelist, Howells was always caught in the critical debate of the interrelationship of writer's aesthetic and his craft. In *Their Wedding Journey*, Howells has given expression to this critical dilemma in light-hearted satire, but that dilemma remains incomplete in its expression and finds a more complete expression in *A Hazard of New Fortunes*, when both Basil and Isabel have matured not only in years but also in ethical and social understanding. Jerome Klinkowits has also traced this conflict of "Ethic and Aesthetic" in the March narratives and has observed that "there exists in the March stories a theme that begins in *Their Wedding Journey*, contributes a major statement in *A Hazard of New Fortunes,* and goes on toward even more depth and complexity in minor works of 1890s."[24] The wedding journey of Isabel and Basil has all the attractions of aesthetic and romantic pleasure, which usually a wedding journey is supposed to have. The hail-storm in the beginning of their journey poses no dangerous threat to them and the prancing and leaping of the horses under the pain of the "stinging blows of the hail stones" appear to them as "neutralists bit of pantomime contrived for their admiration" (*Journey*: 4). Even after thirty years, when they appear once again in, *A Hazard of New Fortunes* the yearning to overlook the moral dimension of the scene and to lapse into the aesthetic pleasure is there in them. In *A Hazard of New Fortunes*, Howells shows that age does not necessarily bring maturity in mental vision and the desire for enjoyment and aesthetic pleasure does not die out. In their house-hunting, which like their wedding journey provides them with an opportunity to watch New York at close quarters, the wish to retreat to picturesque scenes is strong in Basil and Isabel March. On the second morning of their tiring apartment hunting, they try to search once again for the New York of the earlier days and find that "the eye miss(es) the tumultuous perspective of former times."[25] They visit a church, where

> rapt far from New York, if not from earth, in the dim richness of the painted light, the hallowed music took them with solemn ecstasy, the aerial, aspiring Gothic forms seemed to lift them heavenward. They came out reluctant into the dazzle and bustle

of the street, with a feeling that they were too good for it, which they confessed to each other with whimsical consciousness (*Hazard*: 47)

The unrealistic is beautiful and the desire to bask in the unreality is quite strong in Isabel as she confesses: "I wish we did not always recognize the facts as we do. Sometimes I should like to blink them. I should like to think I was devoter that I am, and younger, and prettier"(*Hazard*: 47-48). However, reality they have to face, they are forced to face when suddenly they watch a "decent-looking man with the hard hands and broken-nails" (p. 60) searching for food in the gutter. Seeing this, their illusions are shattered. In fact, just prior to this shattering sight they had been planning not to indulge in any kind of sentimentalizing. "I do not believe", says Isabel, "there's any real suffering---not real suffering---among those people, that is, it would be suffering from our point of view, but they've been used to it all their lives, and they don't feel their discomfort so much" (p.60). But, the sight of the starving man, brings such discomfort in Isabel that she cannot cope with its impact and decides not to stay at a place like New York where "such things are possible" (p.61). In her anguished and tortured mind she again remembers "how pretty and pleasant things used to be turning up all the time on our travels in the old days.... When none of these dismal things happened" (pp. 61-62). It is Basil who ultimately lifts the curtain from such misconceptions from Isabel's as well as the reader's mind:

"It was good deal dirtier", he answered, "and I fancy worse in every way---hungrier, raggeder, more wretchedly housed. But it wasn't the period of life for us to notice it" (pp. 61-62).

It is an implicit confession by Howells that now his social horizon has widened to notice the same moral and ethical lacuna in life, which perhaps either he ignored earlier or his mind was not receptive enough to receive the message of the degenerating and declining human scenario.

Even when Isabel and Basil have entered middle age, both of them share the common impulse to escape the vicissitudes of life. Through the tough house-searching in the first part of *A Hazard of New Fortunes* Howells has tried to establish "March's incipient romanticist-realist conflict."[26] Whereas in *Their Wedding Journey* the same couple could aestheticize and fantasize the actual suffering, in a *A Hazard of New Fortunes* they cannot, even if they want to. Even in *Their Wedding Journey*, the undercurrent of irony is there when the new bride Isabel is shown "deftly escaping contact with a long row of ash barrels in which the decrepit children and mothers of the streets were clawing for bits of coal" (*Journey*: 23-26). So Basil and Isabel's pity which remains "an abstraction" during their wedding journey is turned into a concrete reality in *A Hazard of New Fortunes*. Howells' recognition and enlargement of social and moral viewpoint finds full expression in *A Hazard of New Fortunes*. *Their Wedding Journey*, which remains an "imaginary voyage" turns into a grim voyage in the house-hunting part of *A Hazard of New Fortunes*.

In *Their Wedding Journey*, when Basil and Isabel March watch a man collapsing from sunstroke, they are shocked and horrified, but not moved. "But let us be selfishly thankful that it isn't you and I there in the apothecary's shop, as it might very well be, and let us get to the boat as soon as we can, and end this horrible mild-summer's day dream" (*Journey*: 54-55) In *A Hazard of New Fortunes*, they both have to reluctantly relinquish this selfish impulse. Seeing the miserable spectacle of that well-dressed hungry man, Isabel once again tries to escape saying, "I shall not come to a place where such things are possible, and we may as well stop our house-hunting here at once."

"Yes? And what part of Christendom will you live in? Such things are possible everywhere in our conditions."

Then we must change the conditions" (*Hazard*: 61).

Isabel's cry for change in the condition is, in fact, Howells' cry for reform, which he knew, was an impossibility. "The romance of self-realization" ends with house-hunting part of the novel and in the next part, Howells enters the social and economic scene of New York, for which this novel has been placed with Howells' social and economic novels *The Quality of Mercy* (1892), *Annie Kilburn* (1888) and *The World of Chance* (1893).

The launching of the new magazine *Every Other Week* takes on the centrality of the theme of *A Hazard of New Fortunes* and all the characters associated with the magazine constitute the microcosm of the world at large. Clara M. Kirk and Rudolf Kirk give complete details of how this grand novel emerged.[27] The canvas of this novel is so vast that the picture that emerges is truly life-like. That is why this novel is considered Howells' climactic work and his "most vital book" which displays his most mature vision that is almost encyclopedic.

Did Howells' theory of realism undergo a change? Were his aesthetic principles reshaped that they turned this book into the capstone? A researcher approaches this book with knowledge of its superiority, as *A Hazard of New Fortunes* has received maximum flow of praiseworthy articles, essays and reviews and is one of the most widely read and critically acclaimed novel. After examining this book, one realizes that Howells' realistic postulates did not undergo a major change. There never remained much scope for his realism to grow or mature, which, from the beginning of his literary career, had firm contours and a full-fledged shape. If Howells shows a mature vision in *A Hazard of New Fortunes*, it is not in his realism that he grows, it is in his understanding of human and social context that he shows his maturity. As Borus comments: "Combining a new emphasis on characterization, some variant of material or social determinism, and a new set of representation techniques his realism aspired to draw a living map of new society."[28] Howells, in this book shows that he could not longer adhere to the ghost of smiling aspects alone and his realistic horizon began to include much graver and serious matters of American life.

By the time Howells was writing *A Hazard of New Fortunes*, his mind was heavily surcharged with the personal misery caused by his eldest daughter Winifred's death, and the impact of Tolstoy on his mind was so strong, which he expressed as "carry me beyond myself and miserable idolatories of the past."[29] It is perhaps, by putting on the mask of fiction that Howells realized his tortured self fully. There is a strong streak of fatalism in this novel and a sad acceptance of chance, which is perhaps not present in so acute a form in other novels. This also accounts for the pessimistic note of this novel. William McMurry, in his analysis of *A Hazard of New Fortunes*, has drawn repeated attention towards the tone of determinism which according to him is also perhaps "a divine predestination."[30]

There are various instances in the novel where the operation of chance and the force of the "individual volition" dictate the life of the characters. Hardy's providence seems to be lurking in this novel from the beginning, but unlike Hardy, Howells does not escape into the realm of tragedy, because Howells knew that that would give an unrealistic turn to his novel. Howsoever sad or pessimistic Howells may be, he never missed the opportunity to puncture the balloon of unreality. Conrad Dryfoos' accidental death by a stray bullet and afterwards Lindau's death do give a sad tone to this novel, but it does not transform it into a tragedy. Life goes on. We are told in the end that Dryfoos leaves the ownership of the magazine to Fulkerson and Basil March and himself settles in Europe. "There the Dryfooses met with the success denied them in New York, many American plutocrats must await their apotheosis in Europe, where society has them, as it were, in translation" (*Hazard*: 430). Even the character of Augus Beaton is shown to possess Hamlet-like indecisiveness. His "momentary qualms of conscience" and "lack of the essential spark of disinterested love"[31] make him a pathetic figure who has all the makings of a tragic figure, but Howells does not allow him to rise to that grandeur, and in the end Beaton too, like his other counterparts in Howells fiction "....laughed with cynical recognition of the fact that he had got his punishment in the right way and that his case was not to be dignified into tragedy" (p. 427).

For Howells, the 'truth value' of realism was the most important facet of his theory and 'fidelity' was his norm which he strictly followed. Though the absence of slums, poverty and pain in Howells' fiction has made him the target of severe criticism at times, yet, Howells could not depict in his fiction that which he himself was not well acquainted with. The scenes scattered in his novels, where he shows direct contact with the poor and the problems of poverty are out of his personal experience. Even Howells' social criticism operates on a moral level alone as he did not possess that deeper knowledge of a socialist critic. Bennett's argument, in this regard is convincing, as it is based on careful analysis of Howells' own confessions scattered in his critical writings and autobiography:

> Howells had already made it clear that he looked to such social philosophers as Lawrence Gronlund for programs and solutions. The record of his public and private utterances before and after *A Hazard of New Fortunes* indicate that he found fully satisfactory solutions about the proposals of Marxian and socialistic thinkers.[32]

In *A Hazard of New Fortunes* which has been placed on a high pedestal of Howells' work, we do get the glimpse of the pain of readjustment to the briskly changing American scenario. It is born out of Howells' true experience, the hazard of adjustment which he and his wife faced in New York. This novel is also considered to be a "narrative of settlement" as it starts with the real search for an apartment by the now-mature and middle-aged Basil and Isabel, who have been referred to as fictive correlatives of the writer and his wife.

The apartment-hunting scene has been criticized for being too elaborate due to its excessive detail. Everett Carter has given in detail the reasons for this technical lapse. One of the reasons for the unwieldy size of this chapter was perhaps because Howells was "striving to get some of its vast, sprawling, teeming life into fiction."[33] Twenty years after the publication of *A Hazard of New Fortunes* Howells himself declared apologetically: "In my zeal for truth I did not distinguish between reality and actuality in this or other matters."[34] Though the repeated criticism made Howells declare and apologize for his error in mistaking reality for actuality, Amy Kaplan views this deliberate detailing as a feature of Howellsian realism:

> In Howells' literary criticism, "realism" emerges as an elaborate balancing act, it reconciles social diversity within an overarching community, assimilates disparate facts to a commonsense morality, and frames a plentitude of details within a coherent form.[35]

A Hazard of New Fortunes is considered as the climax of Howells' literary career due to the multiplicity of themes which overlap and intermingle to form a coherent whole. In Jacob Dryfoos and Berthold Lindau, Howells presents us with the two antithetical extremes of the novel and he works on the theme of placing the socially divergent groups on the level of operations and shows that social diversity marks the reality of the human world. He does not bring any reconciliation between the opposing extremes and does not mislead us into the hope of heterogeneous society turning into a clean, beautiful homogeneous one. Fulkerson is the person who, in *A Hazard of New Fortunes*, tries to maintain a balance between intellectually as well as socially heterogeneous groups and tries to avoid the possible confrontation, because his main aim is to see the success of *Every Other Week* as it is his invention. But he, along with Basil, are unable to reconcile the diversity of thoughts that operate in the minds of different characters and thus as is usual with the majority of Howells' novels, it ends on an open note, which, once again, has been viewed as a technical flaw in the novel by many critics. Bennett, on the contrary, defends Howells' deliberate open-ending as,

> ...appropriate dramatic ironies in which the suspension of clear cut significance is the meaning and realistic resolution.[36]

By the late nineties, when Howells had reached the peak in the direction of realism, his disenchantment with the naked and ugly face of reality was complete. Somewhere between Haymarket and the Columbian Exposition of 1893, Howells completely lost faith in the smiling aspects of American experience. Since he had staked his career on realism, he could do nothing, but silently chart the American life, declining on every front. As Alfred Kazin also suggests: "He had experienced the transformation of American life after the Civil War almost as a personal disaster, and his novels now became the record of that experience."[37]

Notes

1. H.L. Mencken, "The Dean" in *Howells: A Century of Criticism*, ed. Kenneth E. Eble (Dallas: Southern Methodist University Press, 1962): 95.
2. During 1920s quite a number of writers and critics rose in a kind of revolt against Howells' domination in American literary field. They have collectively been referred to as the 'twenties debunkers' and their derogatory comments greatly harmed Howells' reputation. Prominent among these detractors were Sinclair Lewis, Atherton, H.L. Mencken, John Macy and Van Wyck Brooks.
3. John Updike, "Howells as Anti-Novelist", *New Yorker* 63 (13 July, 1987): 87.
4. Jerry Herron, "Howells On My Mind: Reflections on Dean's Sesquicentennial", *New England Quarterly*, 61 (1988): 198.
5. Wayne C. Booth, *The Rhetoric of Fiction*, (Chicago: University of Chicago Press, 1961): 23.
6. William Dean Howells, *Criticism and Fiction and Other Essays*, ed. Clara M. Kirk and Rudolph Kirk (New York: University Press, 1959): 15, 38.
7. Herron, Ibid: 186.
8. William Dean Howells, *My Literary Passions* (New York: Harper, 1910): 186.
9. William Dean Howells, *Life in Letters* (Garden City: Doubleday, 1928): 121.
10. Kenneth E. Eble, *William Dean Howells* 2nd ed. (Boston: Twayne, 1988): 39.
11. Alfred Kazin, *On Native Grounds: An Interpretation of Modern American Prose Literature* (New York: Harcourt, 1942): 40.
12. Alfred Habegger, *Gender, Fantasy and Realism in American Literature* (New York: Columbia University Press, 1982): 67.
13. Percy Lubbock, ed., *The Letters of Henry James* (London: 1920): 1, 30, 31.

14. George N. Bennet, *W.D. Howells: The Development of a Novelist* (Norman: University of Oklahoma Press, 1959): 17.
15. Olov, W. Fryckste, *In Quest of America: A Study of Howells' Early Development as a Novelist* (Cambridge: Harvard University Press, 1958): 84.
16. William Dean Howells, *Their Wedding Journey* (Boston, James R. Osgood and Company, 1872): 86-87. Subsequent reference to this edition, abbreviated as *Journey*, will appear in the text.
17. George C. Carrington, Jr., *The Immense Complex Drama: The World and Art of the Howells Novel* (Ohio: State University Press, 1966): 58.
18. Allen F. Stein, *After the Vows Were Spoken: Marriage in American Literary Realism* (Columbus: Ohio State University Press, 1984): 22-23.
19. Marrion W. Cumpiano, "The Dark Side of *Their Wedding Journey*", *American Literature*, 40 (Jan. 1969): 22-23.
20. John E. Bassett, "A Heart of Ideality in My Realism", and Other Essays on Howells and Twain (West Cornwell: Locust Hill Press, 1991): 58.
21. Kenneth Seib, "Uneasiness at Niagra: Howells' *Their Wedding Journey*", *Studies in American Fiction*, 4 (1976):23.
22. For further details consult John K. Reeves, "The Limited Realism of Howells' *Their Wedding Journey*". PMLA, 77 (1962): 617-28 and David L. Frazier. "*Their Wedding Journey*: Howells' Fictional Craft". *The New England Quarterly* 42 (1969): 323-49.
23. Charles L. Campbell, "Realism and the Romance of Real Life: Multiple Fictional Worlds in Howells' Novels", *Modern Fiction Studies* 16 (1970): 293.
24. Jerome Ilinkowitz. "Ethic and Aesthetic: The Basil March Stories of William Dean Howells" *Modern Fiction Studies* 16 (1970): 303-304.
25. William Dean Howells, *A Hazard of New Fortunes* (New York: New American Library, 1965): 47. Subsequent references to this edition, abbreviated as *Hazard*, will appear in the text.

26. Kermit Vanderbilt, *The Achievement of William Dean Howells: A Reinterpretation* (Princeton: Princeton University Press, 1962): 155.
27. Clara M. Kirk and Rudolf Kirk, *William Dean Howells* (New York: Twayne, 1961): 115.
28. Daniel H. Borus, *Writing Realism: Howells, James and Norris in the Mass Market* (Chapel Hill: University of North Carolina Press, 1989): 19.
29. William Dean Howells, *Life in Letters*, ed. Mildred Howells (New York: Doubleday, 1928): 408.
30. William Mcmurray, *The Literary Realism of' William Dean Howells* (Carbondale: Southern Illinois University Press, 1967): 70.
31. Everett Carter, *Howells and the Age of Realism* (Philadelphia: Lippincott, 1954): 209.
32. George N. Bennett, *The Realism of William Dean Howells 1889-1920* (Nashville: Vanderbilt University Press, 1973).
33. Carter, 204.
34. William Dean Howells, *Representative Selections* (New York: American Book Company, 1950): 239.
35. Amy Kaplan, "The Knowledge of the Line: Realism and City in Howells' *A Hazard of New Fortunes*" *PMLA*, 101 (1986):70.
36. Bennett, *Development*: 34.
37. Kazin, 38.

4

Immense Complex Drama

Howells' novels of the 1880s are a sudden departure from the novels of the 1870s. The novels written during this crucial 1980s phase mark the peak of his career as a literary artist. The discernible twist during this decade is, as Carrington suggests, that "Howells swings away from his belief that being 'downright' is a primitive and natural talent, toward the belief that it is a precariously balanced training and vision."[1] *A Modern Instance* written in 1881, shortly after the publication of *The Undiscovered Country*, has a close resemblance to the latter, as far as the father-daughter relationship is concerned. Marcia and her father, Squire Gaylord, a lawyer and the leading citizen of his town, Equity, in Maine, have strong emotional ties (more than usual) which have been interpreted by recent critics as symptomatic of the Electra complex, just as Dr. Boynton has with his daughter Egeria, in *The Undiscovered Country*. Apart from this, the daughter's attachment to another man arouses a jealousy, which is explicit in *The Undiscovered Country* and quite implicit in *A Modern Instance*. Otherwise, there is nothing common in both these novels and out of the two, *A Modern Instance* is much more profound and an in-depth study of human relationships than the other. Elsa Nettles' remark is valid when she says: "The process of social decay evident in *The Undiscovered Country* is more pervasive in *A Modern Instance*."[2] This novel has been considered as the turning point in Howells' literary career and also the strongest and most profound study of human relationships due to the fact that in this novel, Howells dealt with the themes larger than the mere courtship of the American girl. Howells had also found a subject which charged his strongest imaginative response. As it is a penetrating study of the crisis of morality on a national level, its loss is analyzed in every possible human relationship---between father-daughter, husband-wife, employer and employee and between friends.

The usual criticism against Howells that his novels lack that deep and penetrating insight definitely appears misplaced after reading *A Modern Instance*. This novel operates on a much deeper level that any of Howells' novels and works quite contrary to the usual belief that for the sake of the commonplace, Howells evaded the deeper and more tragic realities that touch the human heart. Apparently from a drama of family instabilities created out of Marcia's defiant and spoilt attitude, which land her ultimately in the quagmire of irreversible blunders, Howells takes up the larger issue of declining morality and vanishing instinct of religion in the changing scenario of nineteenth century America. In fact, why this novel occupies a special place in Howellsian fiction is because Howells wrote it prior to the acknowledged impact of Tolstoy, and yet this novel has the intensity of a Tolstoy novel. Howells himself regarded this novel as his darkest picture of

American life and his strongest work.

The Rise of Silas Lapham which is perhaps the most popular of Howells' novels, also presents the contemporary social scene and a true picture of the *nouveau riche* Lapham family---their predicaments and hazards of adjusting to the elite Boston society. Lapham miserably fails to cope with the pressure of guilty conscience, and loses materially. But he experiences a moral regeneration, and the picture of American society is not so dark after all. *A Hazard of New Fortunes* also presents a stark picture of life in the metropolitan city. Most of the characters in this novel have rural backgrounds and they are shown to be misfits in the city life of New York. Yet, the picture that finally emerges is not of a totally decaying society. The degeneration, no doubt, has set in, yet the view that the novel portrays is not so pessimistic. The pessimism of *A Modern Instance* is pervasive, without being overtly tragic. Another novel, which belongs to Howells' later phase, and which has a similar dark overtone is *The Landlord at Lion's Head*. The two novels---*A Modern Instance* and *The Landlord at Lion's Head*---have dissimilar themes, yet the fatalistic overtone and the dark quality of the novels have a striking similarity. Jeff Durgin, the main character of *The Landlord at Lion's Head*, is shaped in the Hubbardian mould, a combination of a practical, selfish, cunning and charming personality. Like Marcia Gaylord, Jeff faces many setbacks, yet ultimately his misfortune does not teach him anything. He does not undergo any moral regeneration like Lapham. Unlike Lapham, he has the prospect of material success and moral degeneration.

The significance of marriage in the fiction of Howells was, to a large extent, due to his self-proclaimed realistic vision. Howells had declared, many times in his literary outpourings, his conviction to present 'poor real life' in his fiction. This 'poor real life' had, among all other human relationships, man-woman relationship as the most prominent. And the man-woman relationship, in an age of Victorian ethos, could be exposed and explored to the maximum, through the legal institution of marriage. Marriage for Howells had a meaning, much wider and deeper than that of being mere romantic idyll. Howells again and again reiterated the pragmatic approach towards it and in fact, warned "... against the danger of trusting to anything like a romantic impulse."[3] In *A Modern Instance* also, Howells has shown the hazard of choosing a partner on "a romantic impulse". Instead, through his realistic vision of marriage he demonstrated that it was more "of the adjustment of temperaments, the compromise of opinions, the reconciliation of tastes."[4] *A Modern Instance* seems to be the most grim picture of marriage. It is, in a sense, a modern instance of the maladjustment of the couple, Marcia and Bartley. In spite of their all out effort, they are unable to save their marriage. They try their best to make adjustments of temperaments and compromise of opinions, and despite their efforts, fail miserably in marriage and are unable to come out of the perpetual "disruptive orbits of unhappiness."[5]

Coming from the village where the comparatively stable and agrarian structure is shown to be crumbling, both Marcia and Bartley turn out to be misfits in the urban and commercialized life of Boston and are unable to keep pace with its rapid and highly mobile society. They become the prototypes of that 'lost generation' which later abounds in Hemingway's fiction. Harold H. Kolb Jr., while writing about the characteristic features of realistic writers, calls them 'agnostics' and comments that their "books abundantly demonstrate the disappearance of the religious instinct."[6] In *A Modern Instance*, Howells, as a typical realist shows this vanishing instinct in the lives of people living in Equity, Maine, and also in the lives of Marcia and Bartley, who are shown to be unprincipled and unruly, as if made of a "coarse fibre".[7] Actually, by the time Howells wrote *A Modern Instance*, he was forced to snap ties with the innocent and simple America, which he had been depicting so far in the previous novels. One has just to compare the absence of the darker and malicious forces in the lives of his characters in his earlier fiction and laxity in moral standards in the lives of Marcia and Bartley to see the change in Howells' attitude towards the moral standards in America.

In the characters of both Marcia and Bartley, Howells has shown the decadence of moral values which was typical of the American scene of the day. Marcia, in this respect, retains a special identity among Howellsian heroines, who are usually beautiful, intelligent disciplined but not as possessive and passionate as Marcia is. Marcia has to suffer, and suffer irrevocably due to her misdirected jealousy. In spite of all her faults and flaws, she cannot be called a vicious character because due to her 'natural goodness' she tries her level best to save her marriage. Marcia's falling in love with Bartley is, in itself a wrong act, for which she cannot escape the blame. It is Marcia, who shamelessly clings to her blind passion and willingly ignores the repeated alarms regarding Bartley's selfishness. The way Howells, in the earlier section of the book, shows the hungry, almost pathetic, immature passion of Marcia for Bartley is particularly commendable. A few of Howells' female characters are very well delineated and Marcia is the perfect example of it. Howells was well aware of this particular trait in his fiction as he commented in *Heroines of Fiction* (1901) that "novelists are great in proportion to the accuracy and fullness with which they portray women."[8]

In Bartley and Marcia's post-marriage life in Boston, Howells shows this American home being 'threatened'. Marcia is shown completely immersed in 'trivialized domesticity.' A mere "salaried employment" is their "common ideal of a provision for their future."[9] "She willingly lived this irregular life with him" (*Instance*: 167) trying her level best to save from economic abyss by putting up a brave and wise front. Marcia belongs to that class of Howellsian women who "support their own identities to artificial roles",[10] the role of a perfect wife and a mother. The way she tries to rise to the occasion of their economic instability and irregular life is pathetic and it becomes almost a mania for her to show her father that she has not committed a blunder. "The future of any heroic action is difficult to manage; and the sublime sacrifice of her pride and all the conventional proprieties which Marcia had made in giving herself to Bartley was inevitably tried by the same sordid tests that every married life is put to" (p.171).

Though *A Modern Instance* has been considered as the darkest of all novels, the characters in it are not evil incarnates. George Perkins' assessment is perhaps appropriate when he says that in this novel, Howells depicts a "culture as yet incompletely spoiled by materialism (later he would do that, too)."[11] Even in Bartley, who has been variously interpreted as a villain, the potential for goodness cannot be missed. That he, being an orphan, has learnt the tricks of the trade by misfortune of his situation, is still excusable in his misbehavior. We are told that:

> It had been his fortune to be left, when very young, not only orphan, but an extremely pretty child, with an exceptional aptness for study, and he had been better cared for than if his father and mother had lived. He had been not only well housed and fed, and very well dressed, but pitied as an orphan, and petted for his beauty and talent, while he was always taught to think of himself as a poor boy, who was winning his way through the world (*Instance*: 65).

Bartley's smartness, efficiency and intelligence is rather a positive and admirable feature of his character and his lack of moral discipline and selfish sensuality is not an unpardonable sin as Marcia's lack of self control is. Critics like Darrel Abel consider that "lack of supporting tradition"[12] in case of Marcia Gaylord being responsible for the lack of moral discipline in her. Because she grew up in an atmosphere which was spiritually barren, that she fell madly in love with the first man who came into her life and committed the blunder of a runaway marriage. For Bartley Hubbard, "her adoration flattered his self-love to the same intensity and to something like the generous complexion of her worship" (*Instance*: 42). The broken engagement in the beginning is a chance reminder to both of them of their incompatibility. Bartley's easy manner with Hannah Morrison is a stark exposition of his amorous nature and Marcia's reaction of returning the engagement ring is a clear revelation of her possessive and jealous temperament. Bartley is "wounded more in his conceit than in his affection",[13] after the broken engagement, but for Marcia, it is a matter too difficult to be swallowed like that. Ultimately she gives into her passion for Bartley and decides to marry him secretly.

Initially, the Hubbards establish themselves very successfully in the Boston atmosphere. Bartley's quick intelligence is adequately paid for and he soon gets into the journalistic fraternity of Boston and becomes the managing editor of *The Boston Events*. There is a quick rise in their social fortune and they enjoy the brief span of domestic happiness when Marcia gives birth to Flavia, who becomes the center of their love. But this easily earned happiness is short-lived, as the fatal lack of principle from which Bartley suffers, recurs again. Perkins has attributed the cause of Bartley's degeneration to the "city pressure".[14] This perhaps is partly true, because although the seeds of moral disintegration were always present in

Bartley, yet the role of city in expediting the process of disintegration also cannot be ignored.

The economic pressures too play a vital role in the collapse of their marriage. In his news-papering Bartley starts using unethical means without any qualms of conscience, but Howells makes us see in the course of the novel, that the use of unethical means by Bartley is also due to an urge to see and make Marcia happy. The economic compulsions in the expensive life of the city may be an indirect cause of the moral decay in Bartley and Marcia's life. In spite of all this, none of the Hubbards' transgressions are likely to strike a modern reader as being desperately wicked. In this respect, Bartely's own feeling that "he was punished out of all proportion to his offence" (*Instance*: 80) is not wholly incorrect. Bartley Hubbard's misfortune reminds us of Henchard's misfortune and gives us a feeling that chance, in this particular novel also had a dominant role to play.

Bartley uses his weapon of 'slick affability', which instead of proving a ladder to social heights, becomes a mire of failures in which he keeps sinking, slowly but surely. A gradual degeneration sets in the life of Marcia and Bartley, and Howells, with his subtle realistic touches, shows us that both are to be blamed for it.

In the course of the novel Howells' determinism intervenes which gives the impression that they are not to be totally blamed for it. At many places in the novel chance and fate intervene to make matters worse. Bartley does indulge in nefarious practices and his publishing Kinney's article is a wrong gesture, but unluckily he earns an unnecessarily bad reputation. He decides to patch up with Marcia and confesses to her all his misdeeds and tries to restart a good life, but right at that moment when he is fully repentant, Marcia comes in with the charge of infidelity and again accuses him of an illicit affair with Hannah Morrison. "The idiotic penitent that he had been a few moments ago, the soft, well meaning dolt, was so far from him now as to be scarce within the reach of his contempt... the Devil was in him, and the Devil is fierce and proud, and knows how to make many base emotions feel like a just self-respect" (*Instance*: 320-21). Thus, Bartley goes away, very reluctantly though, and when, while catching the train he once again feebly thinks of returning, he loses his purse and his fate is sealed forever. "Now he could not return, nothing remained for him but the ruin he had chosen" (p.328).

Howells, with his realistic touch, shows that their separation is not a premeditated and a calculated move on the part of Bartley. In fact, not even once Bartley shows any inclination for separation from Marcia, who had left Bartley on the spur of the moment. She comes back, hoping against hope that Bartley would come back. But he does not come. For almost two years Marcia is not reconciled to the fact that Bartley Hubbard has left her until Ben Halleck shows her an Indiana newspaper in which Bartley had advertised that he had filed divorce proceedings against her on the ground of desertion. Squire Gaylord and Hallecks are anxious to refute this charge and they decide to go to Tecumseh and file a counter suit against Bartley for seeking divorce from Marcia's side. After many dramatic incidents, Bartley and Marcia are divorced, though the lives of both are ultimately ruined. Bartley Hubbard is shot dead by an angry citizen who had been libeled in one of Bartley's articles and Marcia lives a life of shrunken anonymity, returning to her home town Equity in Maine. Ben Halleck, who had been a silent admirer and secret lover of Marcia is ultimately unable to decide whether he should propose to Marcia or not. He writes to Atherton for advice who thinks that Ben Halleck's love for Marcia, even when she was married to Bartley Hubbard, is in itself "an indelible stain" even if this love remained an unexpressed frustrated desire.

In the end it is not made clear to the reader whether Marcia and Ben get married or not. Much has been said regarding the hyper-moralistic conclusion of the novel which according to William M. Gibson is "ironic, anticlimactic and open."[15] William McMurry, who analyzes the novel on the "motive-deed issue", comments regarding the ending of the novel that "what the novel does conclude is that human pretensions to absolute law and justice, when not checked by an awareness of the limits of human knowledge, are unrealistic."[16]

In *A Modern Instance*, Howells no doubt shows us the face of suffering humanity caught in the web of the motive-deed dilemma. In case of Bartley, he suffers not because his motives and intentions are wrong. His tragedy lies in his actions and deeds, even when his motives are not bad. A clear example of this is when in the beginning of the novel Bartley's one blow makes Henry Bird suffer from a concussion. This action, in which he did not mean to hurt Henry Bird in the way he is hurt, is a great setback to his reputation at Equity.

Everett Carter considers the degeneration and decay of the marriage of Bartley Hubbard and Marcia Gaylord due to its (marriage) being based on "physical attraction".[17] Though throughout his fiction, Howells never comments explicitly on the sexual attraction between the opposite sexes, there are various implicit hints which reveal the use of sexual terminology by him, the lack of which Howells has been mostly accused of. That Marcia's attraction for a man like Hubbard is purely physical is reiterated again and again in the novel in suggestive terms. From the very beginning Howells' comments about Marcia and Bartely's love are suggestive of naked sexual impulses. "Their talk was for the most part frivolous, and their thoughts ephemeral" (*Instance*: 46).

In fact, before Bartley and Marcia are engaged, it appears that it is Marcia who proposes to Bartley and it is she who first makes the confession of love and Bartely gets involved willy-nilly. Marcia's shameless and also innocent confession to Bartley is almost pathetic:

> That is what I wanted you to tell me. Did you ever---did you use to be afraid sometimes that I---that you---did you put off telling me that you cared for me so long because you thought, you dreaded---Oh, I don't see what I can ever do to make it up to you if you did! Were you afraid I didn't care for you"?
>
> "No !" shouted Bartley. She had risen and stood before him in the fervour of her entreaty.
>
> ..... while he laughed, and laughed again. "I knew you were dead in love with me from the first moment" (*Instance*: 47)

In the delineation of her character Howells cleverly displays the anguish which many women silently bear, as they simply cannot come out openly with their agony. Marcia's dilemma is the dilemma of all those women, who commit a blunder on an impulse, and who cannot acquit themselves of that blunder, because that is of their own choice. Kenneth E. Eble quotes a passage from Euripides' plays as translated by E.P. Coleridge which is very appropriate as far as the impact which it seems to have made on Howells' writing of *A Modern Instance*:

> Of all things that have life and sense we women are the most hapless creatures; first must we buy a husband at a great price, and o'er ourselves a tyrant set which is an evil worse than the first, and herein lies the most important issue, whether our choice be good or bad. For divorce is not honourable to women, nor can we disown our lords.[18]

Wallace Brockway's assessment that Marcia's splendor and grandeur has deliberately not been equaled to the Greek heroine Medea by Howells because he wanted her portrayal to be ironical is correct to a great extent. Howells' expertise in delineating, so completely, Marcia's character, her intense passion, her profound grief, her suffering and her silent retreat, which is so genuine, is remarkable. Crowley's remark is perhaps close to the truth when he says: "Howells' imaginative mediation between polarized gender ideals deepened his identification with women, his compassion for their suffering."[19]

But that also did not prevent Howells from portraying a true picture of women. Their suffering and their misfortune, never let him lose his firm control on his realism. He was in fact charged for not portraying a noble, perfect woman for which he answered: "I think that women, as a rule, are better and nobler than men, but they are not perfect."[20]

In *A Boy's Town* written some ten years after *A Modern Instance* Howells confesses the lack of clear perspective in his earlier religious life at Ohio. The same kind of blurred and unclear conception of religion can be seen in the life of people at Equity, especially in the life of Marcia. In fact, in a sense, *A Modern Instance* can also be treated as a conflict between new liberalism, as symbolized by Marcia's character and the old established, orthodoxy as symbolized in Squire Gaylord. Kermit Vanderbilt has given an extensive documentary on Howells' religious comments in Howells' various articles.[21] From still another perspective the cause of Marcia's moral instability lies in the decline of religious orthodoxy in Equity and the birth of new liberalism which is in an infantile stage of confusion in post-war America. Howells, through subtle hints, shows how the "chaotic liberality" of Equity, the Squire's rigidity as a skeptic and disciple of Puritanism, and Mrs.

Gaylord's total loss of religious sense, has been, to a great extent responsible to create that moral vacuum in Marcia's life, in which she has lost all sense of religious direction and motivation. And to make matters worse, she falls upon a person like Bartley Hubbard who as a shrewd journalist does not take any religion seriously as he does not want to take sides and hold "fixed theological opinions" (*Instance*: 205). Thus, both the characters suffer due to, what Kermit Vanderbilt says "the anemic religious spirit in America."[22] Yet, the cause of the moral ambiguity in Marcia's character, cannot simply be attributed to such external factors. Critics have traced certain inherent lacunae in her character which are responsible for her ruin. Lewisohn describes her as "a predatory and possessive female of a peculiarly dangerous and noxious kind, drawn with the most vivid energy and impassioned skill—an energy and skill that could spring from nothing less than an experience, personal or intimately vicarious, of the type."[23]

Marcia is a typical example of the age she is living in, which typifies moral chaos, not complete moral loss. In Marcia's case, life has brought her face to face with her inability to perceive, like many of Howells' earlier heroines, but she does not become wiser from the lesson which her experience of life presents. Kitty Ellison's experience from her acquaintance with the priggishness of Arburton's snobbery in *A Chance Acquaintance* leaves her sadder, but wiser. The reader too feels the pinch of their broken engagement, but it is not so pessimistic, because he (reader) knows that she would not repeat the same folly of misjudgment and may be her life would be better with someone else as she is fully familiar with the shallowness of Boston aristocracy. Unlike Kitty Ellison, however, Marcia sticks to her folly and stubbornly resists learning and growing wiser. Actually, Howells leaves no chance for that. Her bitterness is natural because experience of her life is much tougher than Kitty Ellison. She is not only divorced, she is eventually widowed too. The chance of any improvement or change in her fortune is very bleak. If she has remained unsuccessful in dictating her terms to Bartley Hubbard, if she has been a failure in shaping her lifestyle, in accordance with her desires of an average happy middle class existence, she stubbornly pursues this impulse in managing the life of her senile and antiquated father. "He was very obedient to Marcia, who looked vigilantly after his welfare, and knew all his goings and comings, as she knew those of his little comrade" (*Instance*: 416).

Perhaps Marcia is rendered incapable of reaching that typical Howellsian state of self-knowledge which many of his heroines in earlier fiction had reached. What cause does Howells attribute to the moral descent of Marcia and Bartley? Are they presented as most hopeless to suffer the torment of their blasted fate? The conclusion to this complex dilemma is not easy to reach. They are a part of the whole vicious circle of the commercial world of Boston. Sometimes it appears that the degree of their involvement in this vicious circle is very less and based on economic necessity only. Bartely, already an ambitious young man, falls an easy prey to new American business trends which Witherby possesses. At every stage, Howells gives such a twist to the circumstances that he is left with no choice, except the one forced on him. At one stage, he decides to fulfill Marcia's vocational ambition by joining Artherton's law office, but on the way, his chance meeting with Witherby changes his plans. Witherby offers him a lucrative post, and the charm of a secure job tempts Bartley to shift his focus. Security of a good job and good income is enough for anyone to fall into the temptation and there is nothing wrong in it. Witherby is a coarser version of Fulkerson, who appears, much later in *A Hazard of New Fortunes* in which his commercial instinct for profit in journalism does not strike such a discordant note as it does in case of Witherby in *A Modern Instance.* The reason is obvious. The world of *A Hazard of New Fortunes* is already full of such characters, as it has reached that point of no return, when even Howells had given us any hope for its retrieval. The world of *A Modern Instance* is at the infantile stage of commercialism and degeneration and the moral laxity of any character, whether Witherby or Bartely, appears out of place. So the corrupting influence of people like Witherby and the economic necessity does play a role in Bartley's moral descent. Does that mean that Howells intends to mitigate Bartley's offence by giving a deliberate twist to circumstances? This has really created an ambiguity in the novel, for the reader is unable to work out Howells' ultimate message. What is Howells' judgment of Bartley? It remains a moot point, because Howells appears equivocal and doubtful in handling Bartley. The reader is never sure, whether he loves him or hates him or sympathises with him. Fryckstedt[24] has traced the influence of George Eliot's Romola and shown the development of the character of Bartley Hubbard on the pattern of Tito and traced the similarity in the pattern of their moral degeneration. An illuminating comment by Howells regarding Bartley has also put the critics in more confusion. In a letter to Brander Mathews in 1911 Howells says: "I have not looked at it for a long time, but yesterday I read (a) great part of *A Modern Instance* and perceived that I had drawn Bartley Hubbard, the false scoundrel, from myself."[25] Not only does the author seem to be half in love with this "false scoundrel", he makes Ben Halleck, Bartley's direct opposite to be more disgusting and loathsome than Bartley himself. If Bartley is morally degenerate, Ben is presented as mentally crippled (he is physically crippled too). He is another extreme. Though his being silently in love with Marcia throughout, not expressing ever and feeling the guilt is symbolic of an extreme moral uprightness, yet the sexual repression is too much and in fact it starts getting on one's nerves. Even in his presentation of Atherton, supposed to be the moral voice of the novel, Howells creates a peculiar ambivalence. His moral pronouncements and judgment at the end of the novel sound hollow. In *The Light of Common Day*, Edwin Cady comments that as Howells' moral horizon widened, he and his fellow realists turned 'agnostics' who "in time felt compelled to blast transcendence out from the realm of intellectual fact."[26]

It has been a critical consensus that the creative power of Howells as a novelist showed lackluster signs during the last years of the nineteenth century and the beginning of the twentieth century. He could not produce the works equivalent in intensity and seriousness to his major novels like *A Modern Instance*, *A Hazard of New Fortunes* and *The Rise of Lapham*. But one novel, *The Landlord at Lion's Head* stands out, which though written during his last phase, is not only equal, but is more powerful than the novels of his mature phase.

However, late in his life Howells started feeling that the imaginative expansion required for absorbing the vast canvas of American life was not sufficient. The sense of this inadequacy rendered the writings of his last phase restrictive and limited. *The Landlord at Lion's Head* is, perhaps, the only novel of his last phase, in which the question of moral sense comes up with the same intensity as it comes up in *A Modern Instance*. It leaves us with the same sense of sadness as we feel when we read *A Modern Instance*. Moreover, the moral anxiety and ambiguity of *A Modern Instance* is replaced by firmer grasp on the subject of sin and evil in *The Landlord at Lion's Head*. Howells himself confesses to having a great attachment for his protagonist Jeff Durgin, whose character analysis forms the crux of the novel, because it is in the development of his character that the meaning of the novel is built. Just as Howells liked Bartley, and called him his own replica, Jeff is also one of his favourites as he says: "I have liked the hero of the tale more than I have liked worthier men."[27]

Jeff, drawn in the Hubbardian mould, represents the modern American man, who is practical, ambitious and at the same time, stubbornly perverse. But Howells' realistic handling does not impose any kind of burden of Jeff's wickedness on him alone. He has learnt his own lesson from the world and firmly made up his own world-view. The humiliation and setbacks that he receives from his encounter with the so-called higher society, makes him sharply aware of the inferiority of his position. In a way, Jeff's story elucidates the degree to which mistaken values in American society place handicaps and temptations for an individual. An almost similar situation has been created by Howells in *The Quality of Mercy* where the trusted businessman, Northwick turns into an embezzler and he tries to escape from the responsibility of guilt by fleeing to Canada. That the streak of perversity and selfishness is there in Jeff from the beginning, is shown to us clearly when Jeff tries to get a sort of sadistic pleasure in harassing Cynthia and her brother with a dog. Jeff cannot escape the responsibility of his own will and actions, but as in *A Modern instance*, in *The Landlord at Lion's Head* too, Howells creates an ambiguity. The ambiguity in the latter is not moral (as it is in *A Modern Instance*), it is the ambiguity of the point of view. In the novel, we watch Jeff through Westover's eyes, whose unsure assessment about Jeff affects our judgment too. Jeff's defiant behaviour at Cambridge, appears to Westover as steady advance toward decline and he feels pity for him. "It appears to him that the fellow had gone wrong more through ignorance than perversity, and that it was stubbornness of spirit rather than a badness of heart that kept him from going right."[28]

The crux of the novel is to solve the enigma of Jeff's personality. The reader is well aware that Westover's point of view may be biased and one-sided, and that he (reader) has to solve his own equation with Jeff, and Howells, as usual, like a typical dispassionate realist, laughs at our discomfiture, as he does not spare a single clue for us to form our opinion about Jeff. Howells establishes the importance of the point of view from the very start, by describing the mountain-top, the Lion's Head: "If you looked at the mountain from the west, the line of summit was wandering and uncertain, like that of most mountain-tops, but, seen from the east, the mass of granite showing above the dense forests of the lower slopes had the form of a sleeping lion" (*Landlord*: 9). Jeff's personality can be likened to this mountain-top. It has the same quality of ambiguity as the mountain-top has. Even the strength of both---the mountain and Jeff---has a similarity. "Jeff Durgin, stalwart frame was notable for strength rather than height", (p. 39), observes Westover when he meets him after five years. Lion's Head is also notable for a similar kind of strength "the Lion's Head was a part of the landscape, as imperative and importunate as the Great Stone Face itself' (p. 32).

Jeff belongs to that class of Howellsian characters in whom the ties with simple American values have almost broken and in whom the overwhelming drive for money and power has almost provided with indefatigable strength and power. He is a type of unscrupulous American in decadent and corrupt civilization. But he cannot simply be written off as an evil character. George N. Bennet points out that Howells "was not interested in merely showing Jeff, he wanted to understand him. As much as he disapproved of him, Howells did not fall into the easy simplification of portraying a blackguard."[29] There is no denying the fact that Jeff is a bad mixture. When he tries to follow his mother's dreams of becoming a lawyer, he is lost in pursuing other activities and he wastes his time, money and energy to gain social acceptance at Boston. "What disgusted the painter most was that, with all his belief in the wickedness of the fine world, it was clear that Jeff would have willingly been of it: and he divined that if he had any strong aspirations, they were for society and for social acceptance" (p. 63).

The primary focus of the novel is to trace the growth of Jeff Durgin from a young boy to a successful landlord of the Lion's Head. From his childhood, Jeff is shown to possess certain iniquitous qualities, which remain within him always, but which erupt into a fiery passion, whenever he faces some humiliation. It becomes such a stubborn passion with him that the goodness of moral force of any other character, whether it is Westover or Cynthia, remains ineffectual in eradicating that wickedness. In his experience with the social norms of the society, Jeff receives many setbacks, which in turn accentuate the evil in him and all the sobering influences fail to transform him. The first shock of the inferiority of his social position is received by him at Lion's Head, when in one the picnic parties, Jeff's plate is prepared and he is asked by Mrs. Marven to have his food with the horses. There is no explicit reaction of this incident from Jeff, though his mother retaliates by turning Mrs. Marven and her daughter out of her summer hotel. Jeff does not, even once talk of this, even to his mother but it hardens him. Perhaps, the mania to get 'social acceptance' is a part of the reaction of this incident. The non-serious attitude, brings only frustration as Westover observes: "But he had been falsely placed at the start, or some quality of his nature neutralized other qualities that would have made him a lead in college, and the remained one of the least forward men in it. Other jays won favour and liking and ceased to be jays, Jeff continued a jay" (p. 63). Annette K. Baxter, taking up the question of caste and class in Howells' Boston and Wharton's New York, views Jeff's ultimate retreat to Lion's Head as its landlord as Howells' deliberate use of "the device of removal". Says Baxter:

> Social failures like Jeff Durgin have no intermediate Boston milieu into which they can merge, even if they acquire the money and experience to complement considerable personal attributes. That Boston provided no important second or even third-rate channels for the accommodation of its outcasts and congenital misfits is a view supported by Howells' frequent resort to the device of removal: the Durgin's return to Lion's Head, the Laphams to Lapham, and Marcia Hubbard to Maine.[30]

But in Jeff's return there is more a reconciliation between country and city life than has been the case in Marica's return to Maine and Lapham's return to Lapham. Jeff has been, at least a material success and non-adaptability and lack of social acceptance at Boston has not, in any way left him sadder.

Jeff is also placed in direct contrast to Westover, who, apart from being Howells' voice, possesses a strong moral sense and believes in the essential goodness of man. Along with the implicit conflict, there is an explicit conflict and direct confrontation between their worldview. Westover tries to "waken his conscience" (p. 303) but Jeff's fundamentals are clear. "Prosperity and adversity, they have got nothing to do with conduct. If you're a strong man, you get there, and if you're a weak man, all the righteousness in the universe won't help you" (p. 237). Eventually, even Westover becomes unsure of his own righteousness and realizes its ineffectuality. He realizes that Jeff's rationalized evil, does not in any way impede his way to materialistic success. He is successful in seeing his dream fulfilled, he becomes the landlord at Lion's Head. By marrying Genevene Vostrand, he is able to enhance his social position. The reader is definitely prone to form the similar opinion as Bennett has formed about Jeff:

> Howells has no interest in portraying Jeff as satanic or even as the carrier of some kind of blood taint: evil, for Howells, is a matter of the will, as it had always been, and there is no purely voluntary evil among the sane. Voluntary or uncontrollable evil is a matter for alienists and offers no temptation to the realistic novelist, who wishes to address himself to that area of human experience subject to the ordering laws of rationality and therefore to the judgment of moral principle.[31]

However, at the end of the novel, Westover in his moral judgment, does not free Jeff, of his share in polluting and furthering the evil in general:

> Jeff Durgin sowed success, in a certain way and he's reaping it. He once said to me when I tried to waken his conscience, that he should get where he was trying to go if he was strong enough, and being good had nothing to do with it. I believe now he was right. But he was wrong too, as such a man always is. That kind of Tree bears Dead Sea apples, after all. He sowed evil and he must reap evil. He may never know it, but he will reap what he has sown. The dreadful thing is that others must share in his harvest (*Landlord*: 303).

By the time Howells wrote *The Landlord at Lion's Head* he had considerably developed his concept of complicity which he had not developed when he wrote *A Modern Instance*, but the realism is much more stark, in the silent acceptance of the necessity of evil in the pursuance of success.

The Landlord at Lion's Head has been acknowledged by the major critics of Howells as the novel which undoubtedly reflects Howells' best fictional abilities and textual artistry. Although earlier this novel did not receive much of the critical attention which is its due share, recently, it has been adjudged on the same pattern as Howells' other major novels. The pristine Lion's Head and its towering presence and Jeff's efforts to modernise its neighbourhood is, in fact, the artistic dramatisation of the birth of new America on the roots of rural America. "The novel was Howells' strongest effort toward showing that just as spiritual goodness does not necessarily receive material reward in this world so spiritual badness does not inevitably reap chastisement on this side of earth."[32]

Westover, a painter from Boston, comes to spend a week in northern New England, where a picturesque mountain peak catches his attention, for being mysteriously beautiful. Westover's stay at that farmhouse brings him quite close to the family, especially to the lady of the house, Mrs. Durgin, who starts valuing Westover's opinions a lot, as he is, in a way, the founder of their fortunes. Westover comes at that juncture when the Durgin family is deeply entrenched in poverty and have no way out of their poverty. It is Westover who makes Mrs. Durgin realize the economic importance of the location, by making them aware of their house being situated near a good scenic sport (the Lion's Head mountain) which could be a good tourist attraction. Apart from Mrs. Durgin, it is Jeff who makes his presence felt by his sadistically naughty pranks. From a young lad of thirteen, in the beginning of the novel, to the landlord at Lion's Head, "Jeff is decent enough between his spasms of impishness".[33]

During his second visit after five years, Westover is surprised to see a drastic change in the whole set up. Durgin's house turns into a good summer hotel and there is a marked swell in their fortune. Naturally, the economic security has brought hopes and ambitions and Mrs. Durgin desires to see her son become a lawyer by studying law at Harvard. Jeff, pampered by his mother's wishes, is forced to pursue her ambition. He goes to Harvard, only to be more acutely aware of his social position, and instead of pursuing his career, he wastes his energy in getting a place in the social hierarchy of Boston society. In an incident at Lion's Head, where Jeff had been dished out his food in a sightseeing trip, Jeff has already received the taste of the society and the so-called refined people. For Westover, the visitors at Lion's Head had been "the best of American people... such people are refined, humane, appreciative, sympathetic, and Westover... was glad to find himself in the midst of this unrestraint, which was so sweet and pure.. the first aspects of society at Lion's Head seemed to him Arcadian" (*Landlord*: 53). But this 'Arcadian' society for Jeff is definitely un-Arcadian, "the society which pretended to be civilized was just as savage as any of his own most blackgaurdly impulses."[34] This is one of the major realistic undercurrents of the novel. "What one sees is apparently determined by one's point of view" and that "the act of seeing and judging is relative to the person who sees."[35] Jeff seems to possess a personality which at times seems "wandering and uncertain" and at times "solitary and savage" like the mountain peak. Through the symbolic comparison between Lion's Head and Jeff, Howells wants to convey a meaning that no perception of Jeff may represent the total view of his personality. The problem of personal accountability for conduct has been a prominent social theme in Howells' novels, but it has been dealt with exclusively in *A Modern Instance* and *The Landlord at Lion's Head*. This theme has been taken up in *The Quality of Mercy* too, but with a difference. In this novel, Northwick, the trusted businessman, indulges in embezzlement and flies to Canada with money to escape punishment. In Northwick, Howells shows the pangs of guilt and desire for repentance, whereas in *A Modern Instance* and *The Landlord at Lion's Head* it is missing altogether. Throughout the novel, Jeff does not consider any of his actions in the wrong in any way and there is no streak of repentance in him. In presenting Jeff's instance, Howells took up the subject of evolutionism, which was a popular issue during the turn of the century. But Howells, as he shows in the novel, did not have a clear grasp of this subject. Jeff is assured of material success, but the kind of non-serious approach he has towards life, is a matter on which Howells is silent. As Jane Marston says: "Organic links between past and present, as well as between human and non-human nature enable Howells to state symbolically his uncertainty over whether evolution signified inevitable progress, or random change."[36]

The enigma of Jeff's personality remains. He is presented as a "mixed being" like Bartley Hubbard. McMurry's view, in this regard, provides a befitting conclusion to Howells' realistic treatment of his "mixed beings" when he says:

> In his fiction, early and late, Howells saw reality as also mixed: rather than something fixed, single, and pure, reality he found, was complex, multiple, and pragmatically made by men in their continuing experience, in their growing perception of the world and of themselves. What Lion's Head Mountain or Jeff Durgin may be in any final reality is that element of the unknown pervading man's reality, it is the necessary shadow of his being.[37]

Being a realist, Howells did not bring into use any symbol or indirect hint to prove his point. The characters, in his complex drama enacted the roles of true human beings, neither good nor bad. Yet, as human beings, his characters are not ordinary and simple. In their being ordinary lies their complexity and in their complexity lay the truth of human life.

Notes

1. George C. Carrington Jr., *The Immense Complex Drama: The World and Art of the Howells Novel* (Columbus: Ohio State University Press, 1966): 69.
2. Elsa Nettles, *Language Race and Social Class in Howells' America* (Lexington: University Press of Kentucky, 1988): 131.
3. W.D. Howells, *Their Silver Wedding Journey* (New York: Harper and Row, 1899): 156.
4. W.D. Howells, *The Day of Their Wedding Journey* (New York: Harper, 1896): 86-87.
5. Allen F. Stein, "William Dean Howells" *After the Vows Were Spoken: Marriage in American Literary Realism* (Columbus: Ohio State University Press, 1984): 21.
6. Harold H. Kolb Jr., *The Illusion of Life: American Realism as a Literary Form* (Charlottesville: University Press of Virginia, 1969): 95.
7. Oscar W. Firkins, *William Dean Howells: A Study* (New York: Russel, 1963): 10.
8. W.D. Howells, *Heroines of Fiction*, 2 Vols. (New York: Harper, 1901) 1: 190.
9. William Dean Howells, *A Modern Instance* (New York: New American Library, 1964): 162. Subsequent references to this edition will appear abbreviated as *Instance* in the text.
10. Bremer, 217.
11. George Perkins, "*A Modern Instance*: Howells' Transition to Artistic Maturity", *New England Quarterly*, 47 (September 1974): 427.
12. Darrel Abel, *American Literature*, Vol.3 (New York: Barron's Educational Series, 1963): 156.
13. Abel, 157.
14. Perkins, 429.

15. William M. Gibson, "W.D. Howells and 'The Ridiculous Human Heart' " *Studies in American Humor*, 2 (1975): 38.
16. William McMurry, *The Literary Realism of William Dean Howells*, (Carbonale: Southern Illinois University Press, 1967): 15.
17. Everett Carter, *Howells and the Age of Realism* (Philadelphia: Lippincott, 1954): 146.
18. Kenneth E. Eble, *William Dean Howells*, 2nd ed. (Boston Twayne, 1982): 79-80.
19. John W. Crowley, *The Mask of Fiction: Essays on W.D.H.* (Amherst: University of Massachusetts Press, 1984): 41.
20. Ulrich Halmann (ed.), *Interviews with William Dean Howells* (Arlington American Literary Realism, 1973): 17.
21. Kermit Vanderbilt, *The Achievement of W.D. Howells: A Reinterpretation* (Princeton: Princeton University Press 1968): 52.
22. Vanderbilt, 61.
23. Ludwig Lewisohn, *Expression in America* (New York: Harper, 1932): 244.
24. Olov W. Fryckste, *In Quest of America: A Study of Howells' Early Development as a Novelist* (Cambridge: Harvard University Press, 1958): 245.
25. Mildred Howells (ed.), *Life in Letters of William Dean Howells*, 2 Vols (Garden City: Doubleday, 1928): II: 301.
26. Edwin H. Cady, *The Light of Common Day: Realism in American Fiction* (Bloomington: Indiana University Press, 1977): 8.
27. Edwin H. Cady, The Realist at War: *The Mature Years 1885-1920 of William Dean Howells*, (Syracuse: Syracuse University Press, 1958): 255.
28. William Dean Howells, *The Landlord at Lion's Head* (New York: The New American Library, 1964): 64. Subsequent references to this edition will appear abbreviated as *Landlord* in the text.
29. Bennet, *Development: 207.*

30. Annette K. Baxter, "Caste and Class: Howells' Boston and Wharton's New York", *Midwest Quarterly*, 4 (1963): 356.
31. George N. Bennett, *The Realism of W.D. Howells 1889-1920* (Nashville: Vanderbilt University Press, 1973): 135.
32. Sister Mary Petrus Sullivan, "The Function of Setting in Howells' *The Landlord at Lion's Head*", *American Literature*, 34 (1962): 39.
33. Oscar W. Firkins, *William Dean Howells: A Study* (Cambridge: Harvard University Press, 1924): 69.
34. Cady, *Realist at War*: 228.
35. McMurry, 90, 93.
36. Jane Marston, "The Law of Nature and the Design of History: *The Landlord at Lion's Head*", *Nineteenth Century Fiction* 9 (1984): 172.
37. William J. McMurry, "Point of View in Howells' *The Landlord at Lion's Head*", *American Literature*, 34 (1962): 213.

5

Popular Story Paradigm

That Howells' so-called "placid aesthetic temperament",[1] of his earlier fumbling as a writer was gradually changing into a troubled conscience, is clear from his major fiction of the eighties. Although the acknowledged impact of Tolstoy deepened his social awareness, yet, a closer view of the technique used in these novels reveal many other reasons for the growth of his vision. One more point is highlighted, that Howells' art cannot be studied in isolation from his total experience as a man. Why were Howells' most comfortable and successful years, most turbulent too? The growth of his social inclination cannot be attributed to the impact of Tolstoy or the necessity created out of the spur of the moment alone. The taste of success and wealth, which Howells had achieved, after much hard work, was perhaps another factor, which made him acutely aware of the real social disparities that existed in money-oriented America. One particular thread runs so prominently through his fiction that it might almost be called his leitmotif. This recurrent theme is the confronting of the simple with the sophisticated, the rustic with the urban.

In *The Rise of Silas Lapham*, Howells makes use of two popular nineteenth century story paradigms, the Horatio Alger "success-myth" and the sentimental novel of self-sacrifice, which he weaves together to bring about the inversion of these popular myths. Howells make these two story paradigms the target of his mild satire which ultimately result in a welter of pervasive ironies. The success myth had a deep impact on the American psyche. Its founding father Ben Franklin created an image of a hard-working, self-disciplined and an ambitious adventurer who became an ideal of success and industrial progress, whose road to success lay in his hard work and a few strokes of luck.

In Lapham's story, Howells depicts a man who has already reached the peak of his career. As the novel opens, we watch Lapham, being interviewed by a seasoned journalist, Bartley Hubbard, for the "Solid Men of Boston" series for *The Events*. Silas Lapham is a paint-millionaire, and that the story of his struggles and hardships would be the topic of great interest for American readers is evident from Bartley's interview, in which he mixes the authentic and the imaginary life of Silas Lapham. This is evident from the conversation between Bartley and Silas:

> "So you want my life, death, and Christian sufferings, do you, young man?
>
> "That's what I'm after", said Bartley. "Your money or your life." "I guess you wouldn't want my life without the money", said Lapham, as if he were willing to prolong these moments of preparation. "Take 'em both", Bartley suggested. "Don't want your money without your life, if you come to that. But you are

just one million times more interesting to the public than if you had not a dollar, and you know that as well as I do, Mr. Lapham. There's no use beating about the bush."[2]

The note of popular story paradigm is struck when Bartley says: "...you are just one million times more interesting to the public than if you had not a dollar" (*Lapham*: 2). Here is also an implicit recognition by Howells that non-common man was definitely a more interesting figure for the reading public. Within the dramatic frame of the interview, Howells sets the tone of the novel carefully. Through the technical play of the interview Howells constructs the structure of the novel in a perfect manner. He uses the interview pattern to artistically squeeze the detail of Lapham's earlier hardships on the road to success, inverting the success-myth paradigm. Contrary to the usual Horatio-Alger myth design, Lapham's commercial success to the point of becoming a rich business-man is not elaborated upon. The details of how a poor back-country boy amasses wealth, partly through hardwork and partly through the stroke of luck was not important for Howells. He wanted to break the myth of eternal happiness---'they lived happily ever after' associated with the life of these successful men. With his realistic scalpel, he wanted to dig out the aftermath of success, the humiliation of non-adjustability faced by these poor-turned-rich businessmen. He wanted to uncover the utter powerlessness of wealth in buying a good taste of high manners.

The opening scene of the novel represents Howells' reformulation of the popular interpretation of story attached to successful men. "Howells represents Hubbard's interview as corrupt in intent and execution. His interviewing methods seek to suppress a many-faceted human being in order to fit him into the newspaper's version of human worth."[3] While writing about the interview, Hubbard, very conveniently switches over to the personality-oriented cliche, which he knows would strike well at his reader's imagination.

> "In personal appearance", wrote Bartley in the sketch for which he now studied his subject, while he waited patiently for him to continue, "Silas Lapham is a fine type of the successful American. He has a square, bold chin, only partially concealed by the short reddish-grey beard, growing to the edges of his firmly closing lips. His nose is short and straight: his forehead good, but broad rather than high, his eyes blue, and with a light in them that is kindly or sharp according to his mood. He is of medium height, and fills an average arm-chair with a solid bulk, which on the day of our interview was unpretentiously clad in a business suit of blue serge. His head droops somewhat from a short neck, which does not trouble itself to rise far from a pair of massive shoulders" (*Lapham*: 2).

Howells' interview scene is remarkable for the multiplicity of functions it performs. Apart from satirizing the attraction for externals in the success stories of the day, it also acquaints us with character and personality of Silas Lapham without any overt commentary by the narrator. Howells, as a true realist, laid a great emphasis on maintaining objectivity in dealing with his characters, and through the medium of interview he is able to maintain that objectivity and also reveal the real identity of his hero. Brenda Murphy has traced many parallels in Lapham's life story as written by Bartley Hubbard with almost similar popular paradigms in *Boston Herald* status. Brenda has traced a specific parallel of Silas Lapham's interview by Bartley with an almost similar interview in *Boston Traveller* "Milwaukee's Millionaire". "Silas Lapham was Howells' correction to the notion that 'true history' was to be found in ready-made cultural formulas, and his foregrounding of the cultural formulas was the chief technique he used to convey his correction."[4]

Howells' concern with social and moral issues had undergone a drastic change. We have sufficient proof of this change in his biographies and the detail of his being under the impact of Tolstoy and of his being under the stress of his daughter Winifred's illness which was responsible for that 'bottom-dropped out syndrome' about which Cady has furnished a lot of detail.[5] Howells' novels of this period highlight, that for him, American experience, no longer bordered around the smiling aspects alone. Even the semi-comical situation of Lapham's struggle with proper use of the immense wealth is tinged with a pathetic undertone. The major themes taken up in Silas Lapham, the snobbery of Boston Brahmins versus the innocence of the New Englanders in the interaction of Coreys and Laphams, the exposition of the romantic impulse of self-sacrifice in Tom-Irene-Penelope triangle and the inversion of Horatio-Alger myth, all converged to form a consistent whole, in which the prime theme of moral dilemma is rendered coherently. It is not for no reason that this novel has been placed on the highest pedestal of popularity in Howellsian fiction.

The influence of Jane Austen in the delineation of female characters is quite noticeable in this novel. Irene and Penelope, the two daughters of Silas Lapham, are shown as typically unrefined as far as the standard of the high class culture of Boston society is concerned. But they are completely at ease with the situation and not conscious of anything lacking in them. The strength of their innocence was in this peculiar contentment.

> Laphams had no skill or courage to make themselves noticed, far less courted by the solitary invalid, or clergyman, or artist. They lurked helplessly about in the hotel parlours, looking on and not knowing how to put themselves forward. Perhaps they did not care a great deal to do so. They had no conceit of themselves, but

a sort of contentment in their own ways that one may notice in certain families (*Lapham*: 27).

So, in the beginning of the novel, the innocence of the Laphams is uncorrupted. Between the two sisters, Penelope, the elder one, remains unaffected by the false standard of the society, because Howells informs us, of her maturity of vision in one brief sentence that she "did not care for society" (p. 27). The younger, Irene who is more beautiful, is more vulnerable. Due to the lack of intellect, she has mistaken notions, which are acquired. The obvious contact between the character and temperament of the two sisters, is obviously Howells' technical tool of presenting two points of view, one romantic and hence blurred, in Irene and other realistic and hence clear, in Penelope.

Lapham's chance acquaintance with Coreys in a small summer resort in Canada makes them aware of their social position and their acquaintance marks the beginning of their social dilemma. After meeting the Coreys, it dawns upon them that with wealth, they have to acquire a taste equivalent to their social position. Mrs. Lapham tells Silas about the inferiority complex, which she experiences, after meeting the Coreys. "They had about the best manners, and they had been everywhere, and knew everything. I declare it made me feel as if we had always lived in backwoods" (p. 28). The sincere attempt to make an impact on Boston society starts after the Laphams meet the Coreys, as they learn "a new system for ascertaining human worth."[6] One by one, this new awareness starts unfolding the lacunae of their breeding. Mrs. Lapham realizes that the locality where they are living is not up to the mark as the ladies from the Corey family call on their house and leave with the remark, "Nearly all our friends are on the New Land or on the Hill" (p. 29). The "New Land" has the temptation of

"New World" for Mrs. Lapham and she starts pressing Mr. Lapham for a new house. Parallel to social rise, Howells develops the fable of courtship, which is the subplot of the novel, mostly referred to as love plot between Tom, Irene and Penelope Lapham. In the love-plot too, Howells makes use of the inversion technique. Reversing the usual conventional framework of the boy being stuck by the beautiful daughter Irene, Howells makes Tom Corey fall in love with Penelope Lapham, intelligent but less beautiful daughter of the Laphams. The sequence of events of the novel is so constructed, that even the reader, like the other characters in the novel, expect and await Tom's proposal to Irene as Tom's visits to the Lapham house become quite frequent. Earlier criticism regarded the love plot as an intrusion as Thomas G. Tanselle considered it as "not integrally related to the main story of Silas' financial downfall and ethical rise; it has been considered Howells' concession to the public demand for romance".[7] Early analysis of the plot of *The Rise of Silas Lapham* has chiefly revolved around two issues: the relation of its two story-lines or plots to each other and to the novel as a whole, and the nature of its form, archetype and genre. The most influential views on the relation of its story-lines in provided by Donald Pizer's contention in "*The Ethical Unity of The Rise of Silas Lapham*". Pizer thinks the two plots to be artistically united towards the central theme as he says, "the subplot of *The Rise of Silas Lapham* serves the functions of doubling the statement of the novel's theme, of foreshadowing the moral principle governing the main plot, and of introducing Lapham to the correct solution of moral problem."[8] Howells' inclusion of the love-plot is functional. Through the mistaken judgement, which the reader and the character form about Tom's affair, Howells made the conventional love story the target of his satire. A committed realist like Howells never missed a chance to expose the fallacies associated with romantic notions. When the Laphams discover their mistake, they are thrown into confusion. Irene's heart is broken and Penalope is racked by guilt and convinced that nothing can make their love 'right', a prophecy that she does her best to make self-fulfilling by refusing to have anything more to do with the young man.

The sentimentality of the whole situation is dramatic and self-evident and is indeed highlighted by Howells' implicit comparison with this romance of the novel and the plot of an imaginary sentimental novel much discussed by his characters. The Tennysonian title of the novel is *Tears Idle Tears*, and in the words of a certain Miss Kingsbury: "It's perfectly heart breaking... there's such a dear old fashioned hero and heroine in it, who keep dying for each other all the way through, and making the most wildly satisfactory and unnecessary sacrifices for each other" (p. 211). Boston society, in general, considered such novels as frivolous but harmless, but Mr. Sewell, who has been considered "Howells' moral spokesperson"[9] comments in the narrator's voice, "The novelists might be the greatest possible help to us if they painted life as it is, and human feelings in their true proportion and relation but for the most part they have been and are altogether noxious" (p. 212). Though such calculated discussions in the narrative discourse of the novel have been the part of realistic technique made use of by Howells in most of his novels, in *The Rise of Silas Lapham* Howells' excessive use of these discussions regarding the content of a good novel has made Carrington remark "in a sense, all of *The Rise of Silas Lapham* is an appendage to comments and generalizations... The fiction is inside the essay, which the characters in fiction know nothing about..."[10] The talk of the sentimental fiction in the novel and its harmful effect on the young minds is not merely Howells' technique to illustrate arbitrarily his literary thesis. In Penelople's initial reaction of indulging in self-sacrifice, such discussion has a specific function to perform. We know that in the whole Lapham family, Penelope is the only one who is superior to all other family members in her mature and balanced vision of life. Then:

> What is it that compels a sensible girl, hitherto remarkable for her satiric cast of mind which thrives on the exposure of affectation in others, in herself, in the characters of the novels she reads, suddenly to reject the handsome hero's declaration of love in favour of some melodramatic renunciation of her own on the ground that her sister and parents have assumed mistakenly that Corey was in love with Irene?[11]

The answer to this query as posed by Eakin is in her reading of sentimental novels, which have twisted her psyche. Another reason for her indulgence in self-sacrifice is provided by Eakin for her being "a New England girl, the sort of young woman in nineteenth century fiction to whom self-sacrifice is second nature."[12] When Mrs. Lapham and her husband also discover the news of Tom's involvement with Penelope, they are wonder-struck and realize the mistake of their miscalculation. The situation strikes them as quite hopeless and they don't know how to cope with it. The intricacy of the situation is above their simple minds, so ultimately they decide to seek help from Mrs. Sewell, whom they consider wise in this respect. Sewell views Lapham's coming to him for advice in a rational manner when he says, "we can be of use to one another here, because we can always be wiser for someone else than we can for ourselves. We can see another's sins and errors in a more merciful light—and that is always fairer light—than we can our own; and we can look more safely at other's afflictions" (p. 257). Sewell's expertise in the rational consequences of a circumstance is what Howells wants to convey through the inverted story paradigms. Sewell's suggestions to Laphams, in his famous 'economy of pain' speech advocates "utilitarianism's image of man-the-maker calculating the future balance of good and evil to be achieved by his free acts."[13]

"One suffers instead of three, if none is to blame? Suggested Sewell. That's sense, and that's justice. It's the economy of pain which naturally suggests itself, and which would insist upon itself, if we were not all perverted by traditions which are the figment of the shallowest sentimentality" (p. 257).

The 'economy of pain' formula as advocated by Howells in this novel has been interpreted variously. Too much rationalization of human emotions, as advocated by Mr. Sewell, who acts as Howells' spokesman is the height of anti-sentimental approach which does not appear realistic. But, as Donald Pizer suggests, "the ethical core of the novel can be described as utilitarianism" since both the love and business plots "dramatize a moral principle in which the correct action is that which results in the greatest happiness for greatest number."[14] The confusion in the love plot is solved amicably, though Irene is naturally heart broken, but she takes it stoically and removes her unwanted presence by going to her uncle at Duberque. There is a 'rise' among the characters associated with the love plot, not the moral rise, but the rise to the maturity and practicality of human relationships. Thus, as William McMurry suggests, "the love between Penelope and Tom is a sign of the healing of the cancerous falseness which has infected the Lapham family."[15] Thus, through the effective use of intrusive literary polemic, which perhaps Howells had specifically invented for his relentless war against the sentimental fiction, Howells is able to give a proper solution to the love tangle. But, Howells fails in solving the social disparity in the Lapham-Corey tangle. The marriage of Tom and Penelope is no answer to the social inequality, which remains forever despite their marriage. As Howells grew in age, his indictment against the social disparities in socially stratified society of Boston became more severe. In fact, when Howells himself achieved success, he realized that success or wealth did not make him a part of Boston society, which always kept a social distance from these *nouveau riche*. Part of the novel *The Rise of Silas Lapham* is concerned with this struggle by the Lapham family to find a placement in the social hierarchy of Boston society. The building of their house at Beacon Street is symbolic of their efforts to seek a place in 'Boston aristocracy'. The burning of the house is symbolic, eventually, not only of the financial decline of Silas, it is also symbolic of the failure of their effort to get the much desired place.

The dinner party, which is the real, as well as the symbolic center of the novel shows the defeat of the Laphams in their struggle for social recognition. The Laphams, particularly Lapham himself, are acutely nervous on the evening of the dinner party. He hastily takes off his saffron gloves when he sees Tom without gloves, and the evening gets off to a frigid start when Mrs. Lapham, on the point of entering the drawing room of the Coreys' aristocratic eighteenth-century house, bluntly informs Mrs. Corey that Penelope first didn't feel like coming to the party. With much difficulty the Laphams manage to recover from their social gaffe, but nervous Silas again commits minor solecism and is unable to follow the dinner table conversation which seems to be flitting with quick succession from one topic to another. To reduce his tension, he takes more and more wine which addles his brain and he lapses into his customary boastfulness. Tom, who is otherwise not of the snobbish spirit, feels uncomfortable at his future father-in-law's gestures and feels embarrassed. The dinner ends in a fiasco. The dividing lines are drawn forever, though they do not prove in any way an obstacle to Penelope and Tom's marriage, because Howells, in no way entertained dramatic turnings in his fiction. Lapham's lack of culture and taste and the hardships he faces due to his failings have been highlighted in an ironic tone, which is sympathetic too. Arlene Young, too, holds the view that "the ultimate result in *The Rise of Silas Lapham*, however, is not equivocal valuation of the character of its eponymous anti hero. Rather, the play of ironic perspectives deftly works to produce the portrait of a man, who, however flawed, commands the respect of characters and readers alike."[16]

The picture Howells paints is that of a family left completely to itself, because its money has thrust it out of the class it belongs but has not been sufficient to impel it into another. In social terms, as Brenda Murphy says, "Howells implies, success is a disaster."[17] Lapham's struggle with the way to use money is comic as well as pathetic.

> Suddenly the money began to come so abundantly that (Mrs. Lapham) need not save, and then they did not know what to do with it. A certain amount could be spent on horses, and Lapham spent it, his wife spent in rich and rather ugly clothes and a luxury of household appointments... they decorated their house with the costliest and most abominable frescoes, ... they did not know how to spend on society (*Lapham*: 156).

After the dinner party, which has been considered the central episode, the quick succession of events see Lapham ruined financially but also 'rise' in the ethical sense. The reappearance of Rodgers brings the question of sin and redemption to the surface. There are moments in the novel when Mrs. Lapham, who is otherwise shown to be more practical and wise than Silas Lapham, misjudges her husband and suspects his involvement with a woman, who later on turns out to be the daughter of a person who had once saved Lapham's life. Persis, "whose values and actions are warped in Puritanical righteousness"[18] fails Silas Lapham at the crucial juncture. Lapham, while trying to recoup his losses with Rodgers, loses a great deal playing the market. Tom Corey tries to help him out by offering to put $30,000 into the firm, but Lapham, his self-respect too strong, refuses to accept the offer. Meanwhile Lapham's new house, which is not fully constructed, is set ablaze, ironically by Lapham himself and the symbol of his false pride is thus reduced to ashes. When so much is lost by Lapham, then instead of losing heart with the sense of defeat, he emerges strong and does not succumb to Rodger's temptations and is thus ruined financially. Silas' life, ultimately turns out to be the story of "self-deception and self-discovery which begins in innocence and ends in wisdom."[19] In his deliberate attempt to highlight his commitment to literary realism, Howells does not show Silas very happy after his financial ruin. It is clear from Silas' actions that he has, somehow, managed to triumph morally, but that does not mean that there has been some strong moral streak in his character, which overpowered him and he wittingly forsook his fortunes. At the end of the novel, when Sewell asks Lapham, how he feels about the whole affair, Lapham's answer does not satisfy the reader's desire, as the reader wants to see heroic moral rise in Lapham's character. But Lapham's answer is realistic and true. Sewell, like the reader has " a burning desire to know exactly how, at the bottom of his heart, Lapham still felt." "And do you ever have any regrets?", he delicately inquired of him.

> "About what I done? Well, it don't do always seem as if I done it", replied Lapham. "Seems sometimes as if it was a hole opened for me, and I crept out of it. I don't know", he added

> thoughtfully, biting the corner of his stiff mustache. "I don't know as I should always say it paid but if I done it, and the thing was to do over again, right in the same way, I guess I should have to do it" (*Lapham*: 393-394).

In Silas' answer, apart from some inherent, indescribable urge to rise above the temptation, we have a glimpse into Howells' determinism. In Lapham's moral rise, Howells shows us no extraordinary circumstances which suddenly reshape his thought process and restrain him from acting dishonestly in a business deals involving Rodgers and the Englishmen. Confining himself totally to his own realistic tradition, Howells shows Lapham's rise as a result of the simple dictates of the conscience which sometimes do no let an individual act contrary to it under ordinary circumstances. A few critics have viewed Lapham's self-sacrifice as non-convincing, especially in the tradition of the fictional American businessman, who was supposed to be powerful, unscrupulous and avaricious like Dreisir's Frank Algernon in *The Financier*. Andrew Hook has given a convincing argument for Silas' eventual resistance to Rodger's temptation: "It is an utilitarian ethic, infused with moral idealism and a hint of a Tolstoyan sense of brotherhood of man."[20]

Howells took up the theme of current type of American success, at the height of the Gilded Age, but he did not portray in Silas' character, the type of businessman in whom there was any kind of yearning for moral consideration. There is no dramatic change in Silas' character at the end of the novel, when he is able to resist Rodger's temptation. Silas, from the beginning, is shown to possess that moral sense, which though dormant, due to material attraction, has always been there. In the whole range of Howells' characters, there is hardly any character, who is totally immoral. Howells always avoided extremes, as in the case of Lapham also he shows, from the beginning of the novel, a man in whom ambition has not turned into Macbeth-like obsession. He is not immune to the dictates of the conscience. Howells provides us with a hint in the interview scene at the beginning when Silas mentions his ex-partner, "Well, I had to come to it. I took a partner." Lapham dropped the bold blue eyes with which he had been till now, staring into Bartley's face, and the reporter knew that there was place for a asterisks in this interview, if interviews were faithful (*Lapham*: 4). Bartley's keen and cunning sense of observation does not miss the expression of guilt, which this ever-bragging tycoon is unable to hide. We immediately discover that in spite of being vulgar, bragging and vociferous, there are certain qualities in him which are endearing and this is what makes him common and real. Howells' obsession with the reality of his characters made him create such people in his fiction who were too real and sometimes monotonous. Howells quite often used the declamatory tone in his novels, as he used in *The Rise of Silas Lapham* too, for which he has been criticized. As George Arms points out, "... the tone of *The Rise of Silas Lapham* constitutes its greatest weakness."[21] But those who find the tone faulty overlook the fact that, sometimes, because of his passion for realism, he had no other way out, except using declamatory tone, as realism for Howells was a matter of conscience. There are many incidents in the novel which are indicative of Howells' literary thesis of realism as a protest. In the course of the novel, Howells contrives, at many places, a discussion in the novel, to put forth his own ideas. Whether it is Tom Corey's comment on George Eliot's Middlemarch or Charles Bellingham's suggestion for a new kind of "novelist who could interpret the common feelings of commonplace people" (*Lapham*: 213), or Sewells' objection to the sentimentality of the imaginary novel, *Tears Idle Tears*, Howells creates situations where he can act as a commentator for his literary intentions. Sometimes, while doing so, Howells is unable to maintain that authorial impersonality, which paradoxically is one of the major axioms of his theory of realism. It seems as if Howells as a novelist and as a firm believer in realism overlaps and muddles the canvas of the novel. Some critics are of the view that in his keenness to promote realism as a 'positive recommendation' he has developed the love plot unnecessarily. They are of the view that the love triangle has been created by Howells to superimpose his 'economy of pain' formula, and that in utilitarianism' lies the ethical core of the novel. But, to consider 'utilitarianism' as the ethical core of the novel, as suggested by Donald Pizer is to narrow down the complexity of the novel. In so many strands, it is difficult to pinpoint the core of the novel. Is it in the reversal of Horatio-Alger myth, displayed in the rise-fall-rise of Silas Lapham, that the 'core' resides, or is it in somewhat comic interaction between the Coreys and Laphams? Is the marriage of Penelope and Tom Corey symbolic of the elimination of the social discrimination? Robert Falk's comment in this regard is worth considering:

> Howells seems to suggest in the marriage of Tom Corey and Penelope Lapham that a hope for the future lay in joining these two classes of citizens. Tom Corey is the mediating force. He possesses his family's superior taste and education, but is equally sympathetic with Lapham's useful and productive ideas of business. And he tactfully brings the two men together and helps break down their reserves of suspicion toward each other.[22]

How far is Tom Corey successful in helping break down the "reserves of suspicion" is difficult to ascertain. In fact, the ending of the novel gives us no definite hints to the breaking down of the barriers of the two families the sensibilities of Boston are spared by prompt deportation of the offending couple to Mexico. Mexico is a country in which the irruption of primitive elements into a ripened social organism is too common to excite surprise (*Lapham*: 326).

In Silas Lapham's life story, Howells exposes the popular myths associated with the lives of poor-turned-rich businessmen of the gilded age. His vulnerability is almost endearing and in his commonplace problems as a father, as a husband, as an employer and as a social being, Howells eliminates the social distancing to which such figures were usually placed. Around Lapham's financial disaster, Howells weaves a story which authenticates the possibility of his moral rise, as Larzer Ziff says:

> that this hearty vulgarian could make such a decision is believable, Howells demonstrates, because commercialism and social climbing merely form a patina on American life. Scratch the patina and, as in Lapham's case, you find the sturdy, honest country boy who will give no quarter in a fair fight, but who will not take mean advantage of even those who can afford to lose.[23]

The format of the inversion of the popular story paradigm was used by Howells in another, lesser known novel *A Minister's Charge*. The novel tells the story of a farm youth Lemuel Barker, who decides to try his luck in Boston after Mr. Sewell of Boston (a character who also appeared in *The Rise of Silas Lapham*) overpraised his verses, not realizing that his rash praise would be taken so seriously by Barker. It creates false hopes in his mind and he decides to leave his village, Willoughby Pastures, where, so far he is leading an uneventful life as a farm youth, along with his sister and mother. He decides to go to Boston with the idea of getting a publisher for his poetry. When Mr. Sewell receives Barker's letter in which he informs the minister about his intention of coming to Boston, Mr. Sewell, who had acted such a clear-sighted prophet in *The Rise of Silas Lapham*, realizes the immense harm that his ill-advice had done to Lemuel Barker. Instead of taking any action immediately, Sewell postpones writing to Lemuel Barker, who turns up in the city. There he realizes that the minister's words were nothing more than a polite conversation and that he has no future in the city. *A Minister's Charge* was the first novel by Howells, in which he developed the doctrine of complicity for the first time, the doctrine of which, he made use of in many novels later, most prominent being *Annie Kilburn*, *A Hazard of New Fortunes* and *The Landlord at Lion's Head*. Mr. Sewell realizes his mistake, but in a passive inaction, he can only talk about it, or sermonize about it, as Atherton does in *A Modern Instance*. When Miss Vane tells him that he should explain clearly to Barker that there is no hope for him, Mr. Sewell says:

> "Yes I had to tell him at last, after letting him waste his time and money in writing more stuff and coming to Boston with it. I've put him to needless shame, and I've inflicted suffering upon him that I can't lighten in the least by sharing."
>
> "No, that's the most discouraging thing about pitying people. It does them no manner of good", said Miss Vane, "and just hurts you. Don't you think that in an advanced civilization we shall cease to feel compassion? Why don't you preach against common pity, as you did against common politeness?
>
> "Well, it isn't quite such a crying sin yet. But really, really", exclaimed Sewell, "the world seems so put together that I think we ought to think twice before doing a good action."[24]

In the world of intentions, when a person wants to do good for others, but exactly an opposite repercussion follows, has been taken up as the major theme by Howells in his next novel *Annie Kilburn*. Annie tries her best to bridge the gap between socially divided Hatboro, but fails, as Howells shows that it is not easy to reshuffle the order of things, whether they are created by God or human beings is immaterial. When faced with the reality, Barker is broken.

> .... at the bottom of all was a simple grief that he should have lost the friend whom he thought he had in the minister, the friend he had talked of and dreamed of ever since he had seen and heard him speak those cordial words, the friend he had trusted through all, and had come down to Boston counting upon so much (*Charge*: 32).

Non-acceptance of the sense of defeat, combined with the sense of shame, does not let Barker go back to his New England village and he stubbornly resists all pressures. The rest of the novel is concerned with Barker's escapades in the city, where he learns to overcome his sense of inferiority. The novel deals with that portion of Barker's life, which Howells had conveniently skipped in Lapham's life. Instead of dealing with the aftermath of success reached at by a struggling rural youth, Howells, in *A Minister's Charge* acquaints us with the misadventures, and experiences of a young man, till the point of success. Feeling betrayed by Sewell, Barker stubbornly clings to Boston. A young man swindles him out of his last dollar bill, by offering him fifty cents for changing the ten dollars and giving him counterfeit money. In the process, he goes to jail once as he is too proud to borrow money from Sewell. He is ultimately sent to the Wayfarer's Lodge, a house for tramps, by a policeman. In the course of his shabby adventures, Barker gets an insight into the squalid lives of the urban poor, an area, which Howells rarely touches in his fiction.

The essential goodness of Lemuel's heart is striking. By the time Howells wrote *The Landlord at Lion's Head*, he had lost faith in this basic goodness as we see, in that novel. Jeff, who is also a rural youth, turns into a cynic, and the sense of inferiority and the insult he faces as a "jay" in Harvard, eliminates in him, the sense of moral responsibility for any harmful act done by him. In Barker and Jeff, Howells presents two extreme examples of the reaction of a struggling youth to the impact of city culture. Lemuel Barker's painful experiences in the city do not let him lapse into cynicism like Jeff. Even when Lemuel suffers without any fault of his, he tries to justify the punishment he receives by finding fault within his own self.

> To be sure, you might say that if a fellow came along and offered to pay you fifty cents for changing a ten dollar bill, you had a right to take it; but there was a voice in Lemuel's heart which warned him that greed to another's hurt was sea, and that if you took too much for a thing from a necessitous person, you oppressed and robbed him. You could make it otherwise, but you could not really change the nature of the act. He owned this with a sigh, and he owned himself justly punished. He was still on those terms of personal understanding with the eternal spirit of right which most of us lose in life, when we have so often seemed to see the effect fail to follow the cause, both in the case of our own misdeeds and the misdeeds of others (*Charge*: 66).

Jeff's reaction, in a similar circumstance is exactly opposite to Barker's reaction. Instead of feeling any pangs of guilt, Jeff's attitude towards moral responsibility is symbolic of the vanishing instinct, which Howells shows present in people in his later works. When Westover, in *The Landlord at Lion's Head*, accuses Jeff of behaving badly with Lyndes, Jeff remarks: "You believe that everything is done from a purpose, or that a thing is intended because it's done. But I see that most things in this world are not thought about, and not intended. They happen, just as much the other things, that we call accidents" (*Landlord*: 189). Westover, who holds just the opposite ideology, which is perhaps Howells' own, is too much affected by Jeff's way of thinking, which shows, that as Howells grew in experience of life, he lost faith in the role of placid goodness. Westover's reaction is a clear indication of this changing attitude of Howells:

> He perceived that in this earth-bound temperament was the potentiality of all the success it aimed at. The acceptance of the moral fact as it was without the unconscious effort to better it or to hold himself strictly to account for it, was the secret of the power in the man which would bring about the material results he desired (*Landlord*: 192).

When Sewell discovers Barker's name and case in the newspaper police report he is badly stricken with guilty conscience and feels responsible for not helping him. He traces Barker to the lodge and tries to convince him that he should go back home. But Barker refuses to go home, Sewell cannot rest in peace without doing something for him, because he feels, he is responsible for Barker's misery. He persuades Miss Vane to take him on as her handyman. This relaxes the tension in his mind for he feels at least he has done some appreciable task for a person whom he had unconsciously harmed. The sermon that he preaches after getting Barker the job as a man servant is good to listen to but not practical.

> He maintained that though some mischief—perhaps most mischiefs—was irreparable so far as restoring the original status was concerned yet every mischief was reparable in the goodwill and the good deed of its perpetrator. Do what you could to retrieve yourself from error, and then, not leave the rest to Providence, but keep doing. The good, however small, must grow if tended and nurtured like a useful plant, as the evil would certainly grow like a wild and poisonous weed if left to itself (*Charge*: 100).

Sewell's' sermon can be viewed as Howells' message because Mr. Sewell is often viewed "as the spokesman for Howells' realism, as the sane, moderate voice of commonplace morality",[25] but, in this particular novel, Sewell's sermonizing reminds us of Atherton's passive commentary at the end of *A Modern Instance*. Sewell's attitude later confirms Eble's observation that, through such sermons, which Sewell preaches so often, Howells questioned "the charitable impulses by which rich Christians preserved their religious principles and kept the poor at bay."[26] In one of the conversations with Miss Vane, the duplicity of Sewell's character is revealed, as it is made clear to us that mere talk of social quality, charity and doing good for others cannot root out the germ of social discrimination which is deeply embedded in American psyche.

> "Oh, she knows it", cried Miss Vane, "We've agreed that you will counteract any temptation that Lemuel may feel to abuse his advantages by the ferociously self-denying sermons you preach at him every Sunday."
>
> "Do I preach at him? Do you notice it? Asked Sewell nervously.
>
> "Notice it?" laughed Miss Vane. "I should think the whole congregation would notice it. You seem to look at nobody else."
>
> "I know it! Since he began to come, I can't keep my eyes off him. I do deliver my sermons at him. I believe I write them for him! He has an eye of terrible and exacting truth. I feel myself on trial before him. He holds up to a standard of sincerity that is killing me... Couldn't you keep him away? Do you think its exactly decorous to let your man servant occupy a seat in your family pew? How do you suppose it looks to the supreme being? (*Charge*: 108).

Meanwhile, Barker runs into a low class girl, Statira Dudley, whom he starts liking and visits the girl's rooming house. One day, when Amanda, her bossy friend, leaves for a moment, Statira stumbles against Barker and he involuntarily kisses her, to their mutual consternation.

After this accidental kissing, Barker rushes back to Miss Vane's and brood over his sin. Due to some misunderstanding with Sibyl, Miss Vane shunts him out, though later on she feels that Barker was not in the wrong, but she is not ready to take him back. In a way, Barker's leaving Miss Vane's job is beneficial to him, as he gets a job as a porter from Mrs. Harmon, the landlady and is introduced to Mr. Evans, editor of *Saturday Afternoons* and a friend of Sewell. Gradually, we watch Barker becoming more citifield and prosperous, but along with it, he also becomes more self-conscious about being in service. He feels more comfortable in the city in many ways, but he feels the pinch of the social distinctions more sharply now. Barker comes closer to Statira and develops a sort of infatuation for her.

Evans visits Sewell and proposes that he should write a sermon, which Evans will publish, on social complicity in evil. The conversation between Evans and Sewell is not only the explanation of the principle of complicity, it is also the explanation of implicit social theme of the novel. When Sewell tells Evans of the harm he has done to Barker and his sense of remorse for his misdeed, Evans, in Howellsian tone says, "what strikes me as being so interesting is that we appear to feel remorse for our misdeeds; and I was almost persuaded the other day by an observer of our species, that remorse had gone out, or rather had never existed, except in the fancy of innocent people; that real criminals like ourselves were afraid of being found out, but weren't in the least sorry" (*Charge*: 180).

Sewell is not content with the way things are happening to Barker. When he comes to know that he has been ousted by Miss Vane, he wants to meet Barker, to persuade him once again to go back and also to hand over Miss Vane's bag. When he meets Barker, he finds him a changed man, to a great extent. After the initial experience of innocence and inexperience, Lemuel develops a tough exterior, which Sewell is unable to penetrate as "he formed no adequate idea of the avidity and thoroughness with which Lemuel was learning his Boston" (p. 187). That Lamuel is no longer an innocent, inexperienced youth, is clear in his mannerisms, yet he is not fully able to grasp the intricacies of Boston society.

> It was wholly a public Boston which unfolded itself during the social intricacies of which it seems solely to consist for so many of us. To him Boston society was represented by the coteries of homeless sojourners in St. Albans; Boston life was transacted by the ministers, the lecturers, the public meetings, the concerts the horse-cars, the policemen, the shop windows, the newspapers, the theaters, the ships at the docks, the historical landmarks, the charity apparatus. He was whirled round and round, he never saw the same object twice the same. He did not know whether he learned or unlearned most with the pride that comes to youth from the mere novelty of its experiences was mixed a shame for his former ignorance, an exasperation at this inability to grasp their whole meaning (pp. 187-88).

So it is only with the public Boston that Lemuel has got acquainted so far. He confesses to Evans his liking the city better than the country, but in an innocent way he pinpoints a particular defect in the city people, who, in spite of having a helpful nature and condescending attitude, have a sense of superiority which he calls "being aristocratic". "Well, at home, in the country, they mightn't mean to do so much for you, or be so polite about it, but they wouldn't feel themselves so much above you. They're more on an equality. If I needed help, I'd rather be in town, but if I could help myself, I'd just as soon be in the country" (p. 189).

Gradually Barker begins to discover social distinctions and

becomes more self-conscious about being in service. Statira now considers herself engaged to him. Through Berry, a bumptious law student, Barker meets Miss Swan and Miss Carver, ladylike art students living there; and comes to admire Miss Carver, who, he feels looks down on him, and this makes him more acutely aware of his low social position. "Once all work had been work, but now he had found that there was work which was service, and that service was dishonour. He had learned that the people who did this work were a class apart, and were spoken of as servants, with slight that was unconscious or conscious, but never absent" (p. 190). He also became painfully aware of the fact that the "stain of servitude was indelible" (p. 191).

When Barker visits his mother in early spring, he feels distant from her but still famillialy affectionate. She warns him against becoming too involved with girls. Depressed by rural squalor, he returns quickly to Boston. For sometime, Howells shows Barker a rootless, alienated man, who is unable to place himself in a correct perspective. Berry assumes that Barker is in love with Miss Carver, while Barker wonders if he really is engaged to Statira, whom he compares unfavourably with Miss Carver. Barker's attraction for Miss Carver and his infatuation with Statira puts him in great dilemma. Since Statira is a also suffering from lung trouble, Barker finds it cruel on his part to detach himself from her at such a critical juncture. Feeling crushed by his responsibility for her, he is most confused about his dual entanglement with the two girls. Firkins has put Lemuel's predicament in beautiful words:

> The uncertainty of Mr. Howells between the competing love claims reminds us of Lemuel's, and, like Lemuel, he temporizes and drifts. In the rapid, almost fugitive close of the narrative, the author seems running away from decisions which he lacks the hardihood to face, and the happiness which he flings in the faces

of the unexpectant lovers at the close has almost the quality of rebuff.[27]

Barker takes his sick fiancee Statira back to his village, where his mother takes care of her and we are left with the feeling that ultimately Barker will sacrifice his love for Miss Carver and marry Statira out of compassion. Mostly, at the end of his novels Howells had to hurriedly twist the endings so that they did not end up in a tragedy. Barker does not marry Statira, but marries some girl whose name is not mentioned and the reader assumes that the girl is Jessie Carver.

Though Barker's life story ends at the point where Silas Lapham's starts, the pattern of their moral and social awakening has a similarity. Both Barker and Lapham have a strong predilection for moral values. Barker, unlike Bartley Hubbard and Jeff Durgin, has not lost all hope in the moral responsibility of man's action. In Barker's various adventures in Boston and in the process of his being citified, he is also not morally corrupted like Lapham. He gives a tough resistance to the evil forces and retains his essential goodness till the end, that radiates and that is partially responsible for his success. What Kaplan says of Lapham, is equally true of Barker. "Throughout the novel, the Laphams are searching for a moral anchor or centre of individual responsibility, only to find their search undermined by the decentered conditions of the world around them, represented by the Civil War and the rise of corporations, which imposes forces beyond their control."[28]

Notes

1. Kermit Vanderbilt, *The Achievement of W.D. Howells: Reinterpretation* (Princeton University Press, 1968): 192.
2. W.D. Howells, *The Rise of Silas Lapham* (New York: Rinehart, 1949): 84. Subsequent references to this edition will be abbreviated as Lapham in the text.
3. Clare Virginia Eby, "Compromise and Complicity in *The Rise of Silas Lapham*", *American Literary Realism*, 24 (Fall, 1991): 24.
4. Brenda, 26.
5. Edwin H. Cady, *The Realist at War: The Nature Years 1885-1920 of William Dean Howells* (Syracuse: Syracuse University Press 1958): 245-45.
6. Eby, 43.
7. Thomas G. Tanselle, "The Architecture of *The Rise of Silas Lapham*", *American Literature*, 37 (1966): 430.
8. Donald Pizer, "The Ethical Unity of *The Rise of Silas Lapham*" *American Literature*, 32 (1960): 324-25.
9. Janet Holmgren Mckay, *Narration and Discourse in American Realistic Fiction* (Philadelphia: University of Pennsylvania Press, 1982): 90.
10. George C. Carrington Jr., *Immense Complex Drama: The World and Art of Howells Novels* (Columbus: Ohio State University Press, 1966): 76.
11. Paul John Eakin, *The New England Girl: Cultural Ideals in Hawthorne, Stowe, Howells and James* (Athens: University of Georgia Press, 1976): 122.
12. Eakin, 122.
13. Fritz Oehlschlager, "An Ethic of Responsibility in *The Rise of Silas Lapham*" *American Literary Realism* 23(1991): 20.
14. Pizer, ibid.
15. William McMurray, *The Literary Realism of W.D. Howells*, (Carbondale: Southern Illinois University Press, 1967): 47.

16. Arlene Young, "The Triumph of Irony in *The Rise of Silas Lapham*" *Studies in American Fiction*, 20 (1992): 45.
17. Brenda, 27.
18. John E. Hart, "Commonplace as Heroic in *The Rise of Silas Lapham*" *Modern Fiction Studies* 8 (1963): 376.
19. Hart, 376.
20. Andrew Hook, *American Literature in Context, III 1865-1900* (Methuen: London): 94.
21. George Arms, Introduction, *The Rise of Silas Lapham* by William Dean Howells (viii).
22. Robert P. Falk, "*The Victorian Mode in American Fiction 1865-1885* (East Lansing: Michigan State University Press, 1965): 129.
23. Oscar W. Firkins, *W.D. Howells: A Study* (Cambridge: University Press, 1924): 115.
24. Larzer Ziff, "Literary Hospitality: W.D. Howells", *The America of 1890s* (New York: Viking, 1966).
25. William Dean Howells: *The Minister's Charge* (Bloomington: Indian University Press, 1978): 28. Subsequent references to this edition will be abbreviated as *Charge*.
26. Amy Kaplan, *Social Construction of American Realism* (Chicago: University of Chicago Press, 1988): 42.
27. Kenneth E. Eble, *William Dean Howells*, 2nd ed. (Boston: Twayne, 1982)
28. Firkins, 120.
29. Kaplan, 42.

6

Romance in Realism

In his autobiographies and articles, Howells openly acknowledged the influence of Hawthorne on his initial writings and his fiction bears testimony to the fact that he was also his follower in his earlier fiction. The romance, as a genre attracted him and in some of his novels, he tried to treat romance in a realistic way. In a few of his earlier novels, like *A Foregone Conclusion* and *A Chance Acquaintance*, he took up thwarted-love between the two lovers as the main plot. In such novels, Howells' gradual shift towards realism is discernible. In *A Chance Acquaintance*, which Howells wrote after *Their Wedding Journey*, and which has been regarded by some critics as Howells' first true novel, he employed the travel structure, to tell the story of the unsuccessful love between Miles Arbuton, a Boston snob, and Kitty Ellison of Eriecreek.

The source of Kitty Ellison's character has been guessed variously by different critics. The most authentic source is perhaps Howells' own sister Annie Howells. Some critics have traced the influence of Henry James' *Travelling Companions* on Howells' *A Chance Acquaintance* and visible traces of James'

Charlotte Evans in Kitty Ellison. William M. Gibson suggests Howells' earlier story entitled "Fast and Firm, A Romance at Marseilles", as another source for *A Chance Acquaintance*. Whatever the source of the novel may be, Miles Arbuton and Kitty Ellison, denot characteristics of Howells' own split and ambivalent personality. Kitty's democratic and independent spirit and Arbuton's repressive gentility are Howells' own. In fact, very obliquely, the novel can also be read as Howells' yearning for a dream world of romance limited by his vision as a realist. In the love story of Miles and Kitty, Howells also explores the social contradictions inherent in American society. The attraction between a Europeanized man and a countrified American woman was one of the favourite subjects for Howells, which he explored in many of his novels, especially the early ones. He used a similar theme in *A Lady of the Aroostook* too, in which he developed the love story within the larger framework of contrasting views of morals and manners of countrified girl, Lydia Blood and the Boston snob, Staniford. This novel too, like *A Chance Acquaintance*, is primarily a romance and Hawthorne's influence on this novel is apparent as John W. Crowley has also compared Lydia Blood with Hawthorne's Phoebe Pyncheon. "Both Lydia and Phoebe come from good New England stock; both are orphans, both find homes with eccentric aunts, both form daughterly bonds with older male relatives; both attract world suitors who refuse to take advantage of their innocence, both inspire the men they marry to reform their ideas."[1] Though the thematic pattern and the plot construction of *A Lady of the Aroostook* and *A Chance Acquaintance* has a similarity, there is yet a vital difference in the treatment of the heroes. Staniford, too, is a Boston snob like Miles Arbuton, but in the end he does not behave like Miles to show himself to be the unmanly man. In the end, Lydia and Staniford are married in the Venetian background "where they blend together as contagious phases of American innocence in contrast to the formality and sophistication of European society."[2] The action of *A Chance Acquaintance*, too, is built on the format of a romance as Howells himself declared it to be a "psychological romance" and once thought of entitling it as "Romance of a Summer".

Kitty, who has been born and brought up in a village, which had a perfect democratic atmosphere, is a pretty vivacious girl with striking western experience and outlook. Its a pity that Miles Arbuton, due to the limits of his social constraint, ultimately loses her. Many of Howells' fictional constructs, like Kitty Ellison, work, not only in the thematics of the novel, but they also have autobiographical signification. Her literary predisposition and dreamy romanticism implicitly project Howells' own romantic leanings, from which he was in the painful process of detachment, as he was committed to realism. The way Kitty is inspired by the "Boston of mysterious prejudices and lofty reservations, that found its social ideal in the old world"[3] bespeaks of Howells' own spilt relationship with Boston, which he viewed, sometimes in awe and sometimes in disgust.

Arbuton, like Colville in *Indian Summer* and Don Ippolito in *A Foregone Conclusion*, is in love, but like both of them, he is indecisive. The immoderate adherence to the code of Brahmin culture does not let Arbuton be his natural self and to him Kitty represents "the possibility of an emotional liberation that is proscribed to his Bostonian temperament."[4] Again and again, he tries to throw off the burden, which his Boston heritage has imposed on him, and through many suggestive hints, Howells conveys Arbuton's secret revolt against the rigours of his social position as a Bostonian. When he spontaneously hurls a pebble at the prison-like cliff walls of Cape Eternity, the sense of freedom and relief which he feels is explicitly shown by

Howells: "It was as if for an instant he had rent away the ties of custom, thrown off the bonds of social allegiance, broken down and trampled upon the conventions which his whole life long, he had held so dear and respectable. In that moment of frenzy he feared himself capable of shaking hands with the shabby Englishman in the Glengarry cap, or of asking the whole admiring company of passengers down to the bar" (*Chance*: 46). But he is unable to continue in his mood of elated liberation, as the inferiority of the position of these people impinges upon his own superiority and he feels himself to be at a "loss with these people, who looked at life in so bizarre a temper, yet without airiness of pretension, nay with a whimsical readiness to acknowledge kindred in every droll or laughable thing" (p. 47).

The novel grows in the uncertain relationship as the romance of the hero and the heroine grow, but ultimately it fails to have an everlasting relationship of marriage. The ending, in which Kitty leaves Quebec and is left to "work out her destiny some other way" (p. 164) frustrated the romantic illusions of many readers, who hoped that Miles Arburton would somehow surmount his false sense of Bostonian superiority and would marry Kitty Ellison. Arbuton tires in the end to overlook everything in the name of love, but Kitty, the practical Howellsian realist decides to end the relationship, when she sees how Arbuton ignores her in front of two Bostonian ladies. When he tries to justify and explain his position to Kitty, her response is most practical and realistic.

> ....it isn't what you've done, but what you are and what I am, that's the great trouble. I could easily forgive what's happened, if you asked it; but I couldn't alter both our whole lives, or make myself over again, and you couldn't change yourself. Perhaps you would try, and I know that I would, but it would be a wretched failure and disappointment as long as we lived (*Chance*: 160)

Kitty's realistic epiphany ends the romance between the two lovers and it is to this sense of realism that Howells turns again and again in his romances.

In his next novel *A Foregone Conclusion*, Howells again takes up the theme of contrasting values. In *A Chance Acquaintance* he had contrasted Boston propriety with western spontaneousness, in *A Foregone Conclusion* he takes up an issue of larger implication. On the surface, *A Foregone Conclusion* has been dealt with by critics as a novel of international theme in which East versus West, conventional versus unconventional are the main issues, but it is also a romance beautifully set in Italian background. It is also a story of Europe and America in which Howells highlights the relative deficiency and merit of both. Unlike the novels of his mature phase, *A Foregone Conclusion* is not a novel specifically contrived to illustrate a point except to bring into dramatic relief the manners and values of Europe and America. It starts as a romance, and would have ended in a tragedy, had Howells not given a realistic twist at the end of the novel. In fact, *A Foregone Conclusion* is the first of Howells' novels, in which he tentatively developed his realistic mode. Set in the picturesque Venice, the story centres around Florida Vervian, a beautiful young American girl, whose beauty enchants an Italian priest. His inadequate understanding of the America makes him misconstrue her free and easy manner as a signal of love. It is not that Florida's beauty so tempts the priest that he deviates from his priestly duties to fall in love with her. On the contrary, Howells shows that he possessed certain unpriest-like characteristics from the beginning, which form the substance of the story. In Don Ippolito's character, as McMurry says, Howells depicts the "continuing conflict between the inner life of intention and spirit and the outer one of actuality. Don Ippolito is able to reconcile his conflict only by accepting the imperfection of his human situation."[5] In the very beginning of the novel, a physician's comment of "that crack-brain Don Ippolito Rondinelli",[6] arouses our curiosity in this priest, who we can make out, is not going to be the conventional portrait of a priest. Instead of performing his ecclesiastical duties, Don Ippolito has invented a canon, which he thinks can prove very useful to the union forces in the American Civil War. He happens to come in contact with Ferris, who is an American consul, placed in Venice, for getting a passport. Don Ippolito, though an Italian priest, is uncomfortable in the restrictive life which his profession has enforced on him. His being an Italian is also, to great extent, a barrier as Fryckstedt observes: "Everywhere there were barriers, political, spiritual, social and economic, they all tended to curb and frustrate the ambitions and the hopes of the individual."[7] As such, Don Ippolito becomes the object of our sympathy as he evokes in us a mixed response as it evokes in Ferris "...he frowned in a helpless perplexity with the case of Don Ippolito, whom he had begun by doubting for a spy with some incomprehensible motive, and had ended by pitying with certain degree of amusement and a deep sense of the futility of his compassion" (*Conclusion*: 13).

For Don Ippolito, America offers striking imaginative response----a land, which he thinks would relieve him from the clutches of poverty, ignorance and exploitation. It is because the American people like Ferris and Florida Vervian, with whom he comes in contact show him the striking contrast with European standards. Ferris' keen sense of observation, is quick to notice this repressed phenomenon in Don Ippolito's personality and he wants to highlight this aspect in his portrait, of the priest, as incidentally, apart from being a consul, he is a painter too, "What I'm going to paint at" he explained, "is the lingering pagan in the man, the renunciation first of the inherited nature, and then of a personality that would have enjoyed the world" (p. 43).

It is Ferris, who recommends Don Ippolito as Italian teacher for Florida Vervian Mrs. Vervian's past experience with Florida's tutors has not been very good, as almost all of them had fallen in love with Florida Ferris is of the view, that with this Italian priest, Mrs. Vervian will not have to face much of problem, because being a priest, he will naturally not commit such a blunder. But in this respect, Ferris is proved wrong. The priest misconstrues Florida's absolute candour and 'delicate unreserve' (p. 87) as an implicit response to his love, as he confesses, "It is in this house that I forget my priesthood" (p. 87). It is this wretched priesthood, that he wants to forget and in one of his weak moments he opens his heart to her.

> How could you know what it is to be priest in this most unhappy city? To be haunted by the strict espionage of all your own class, to be shunned as a spy by all who are not of it... Do you know what it is to have the life-long habit of a lie? It is to be priest... Do you know what it is when such moment as this comes, and you would fling away the whole fabric of falsehood that has clothed your life (*Conclusion*: 88).

In his treatment of this international theme, Howells takes up another important theme of totally divergent attitudes towards truth. In Florida's attitude towards things, Howells highlights an openness and frankness which Don Ippolito admires and envies. Ferris also comments on this aspect of Americans and the lack of it among Italians when he says "they are kinder people than we are but they're not so just, and I should say that they don't think truth, the chief good of life" (*Conclusion*: 101). Although Ferris is referring to Italians in general, the reader finds that it is the dilemmas of priesthood which have been explored at length, in Don Ippolito's life. In fact, as Foster suggests, Howells had "daringly and naively presented the tragi-comedy of decadence within the clergy itself".[8] In Ippolito, Howells presents a confused, chaotic priest, who has been forced into this occupation unwittingly and once he is in it, he has no way out of it. His personal life is full of anomalies. He is lost in his dread-world of bizarre inventions, which he thinks can be very useful in American Civil War. With Florida, he shares his secret of imposed priesthood.

> When I was a child, I used to divert myself by making little figures out of wood and paste board, and I drew rude copies of the picture I saw at church.... I contrived an altar at one end of it, I struck my pictures about the walls, and I ranged the puppets in order of worshippers on the floor, than I played at saying mass, and preached to them all day long.... My uncle... asked me whether I should like to be priest in good earnest, when I grew up. Shall I then be able to make as many little figures as I like, and to paint pictures, and carve an altar like that in our church? I demanded. My uncle answered that I should have real men and women to preach to, as he had, and would not that be much finer?.... I said 'O yes' as children do... I thought... The priests have very little to do, and they gain a great deal of money with their masses and I shall be able to make whatever I like' I only considered the office then as a means to gratify the passion that has always filled my soul for inventions and work of mechanical skill and ingenuity. My inclination was purely secular, but I was inevitably becoming a priest as if I had been born to be one (p.90).

Don Ippolito thinks himself to be more an inventor than a priest. He approaches Ferris with his latest invention---a canon with a hidden charge that cause the weapon to blow up when the enemy captures and tries to use it. But this invention is not practical as Ferris points out to Don Ippolito that it has the obvious disadvantage of the self-exploding cannon---the heat of firing will detonate the hidden charge for the friendly and enemy alike. But Don Ippolito does not understand the impracticality of his invention. He is a dreamer who is not ready to experience the shock of reality, until he is forced to. In his dream world of inventions, there is a suppressed desire of a child who is forced into the vocation of priest. All his inventions seem to have "some fatal defect, they were aspirations towards the impossible, or realizations of the trivial and superfluous" (p. 59). He is, as Habegger suggests "a realist's version of Hawthorne's artist of the beautiful."[9]

In Don Ippolito's frustrating hopes, which he keeps nurturing in his dreams, without taking the adequate action, lies the unmanly man. There are many explicit hints in *A Foregone Conclusion* which convey the effeminity of Don Ippolito who is compared to a girl a number of times. Don Ippolito himself admits his feminine trait when Florida Vervian says to him:

> But surely you can somehow help yourself. Are men, that seem so strong and able, just as powerless as women, after all, when it comes to real trouble?
>
> "I cannot answer. I am only a priest", said Don Ippolitoo coldly, letting his eyes drop to the gown that fell almost like a woman's skirt (*Conclusion*: 94).

Howells who could create such strong characters like Jeff Durgin, whose rugged physique revealed his powerful personality, could also create such effeminate characters like Ben Hallek in *A Modern Instance*, James Nevil in *The Shadow of a Dream*, Miles Arbuton in *A Chance Acquaintance* and Theodre Colville in *Indian Summer* and Don Ippolito in *A Foregone Conclusion*. The range of Howells' realistic world is remarkable in this respect. Perhaps there is hardly any aspect of American life, which he has not explored in his fiction. The diversity of his characterization speaks volumes for the acute sense of observation that he possessed. The character of Don Ippolito had a remarkable effect on Henry James, who perhaps identified himself with the priest as he declares that he (Don Ippolito) is "a figure which haunts the imagination and claims a permanent place in one's melancholy memories."[10] Even in his character portrayal of an effeminate clergyman, as Don Ippolito turns out to be, Howells did not depend on any concocted half-truths. The enforced celibacy and various restrictions had effected the clergy in this way also.

Howells' autobiographies indicate that he wrote *A Foregone Conclusion* under the influence of Turgenev. In it, he developed a "romance that might well end without fulfillment."[11] Entrenched in this particular predicament, the ending of *A Foregone Conclusion* has bitter-sweet flavour, not much relished by readers as usual. Based on the international theme, like *A Chance Acquaintance*, Howells does not follow it with same intensity as he followed in the former novel, because in this novel characters do no signify geographical areas. The European-American distinction, in *A Foregone Conclusion*, is merely a background, on which is built the repressed sexual desire of a priest, which is suppressed, because it is denied.

Just as *A Foregone Conclusion* is among other things "a penetrating study of male impracticality",[12] *Indian Summer*, which Howells wrote almost more than a decade later, too is a study of male impracticality in the matter of love, by a middle-aged dreamer who keeps delaying his encounter with reality till the end. The novel retains a special place in Howellsian fiction, as it is written by him during the period when the social and economic issues had started dominating his fiction so much that romance was conspicuous by its absence. The last of the international novels *Indian Summer* is a "non-social" novel, without any pessimistic or tragic undertone. Eble claims that this book "does not need to be put with or against any other novel."[13] The treatment of the light subject matter at the hands of mature Howells has the desired result of its being a perfect masterpiece. Even the irony in this novel is comic rather than bitter or satiric. A light-hearted, anti-sentimental novel, its construction is such that every action, every discourse and every motive in this novel is explicit. Even if it appears to lack any depth of meaning and motive, as compared to Howells' masterpieces like *A Modern Instance*, *The Rise of Silas Lapham* and *A Hazard of New Fortunes*, it nevertheless retains that complete comic sense which pervades throughout the novel and that is, in fact, the special feature of this novel. Along with the comic sense, *Indian Summer* is truly a realistic novel in which Theodore Colville, who is, to a great extent, a replica of Howells himself, learns to live with the reality of life which he had been shirking so far. The novel also shows that whichever situation or story Howells takes up, he is always fully in command of his art. As Campbell comments: "Howells is the champion of the realistic novel only in so far as it serves to raise people from their false views of life, if another form of writing could do this better, he would gladly adopt it."[14]

From *A Modern Instance* onwards, Howells' interest in the courtship novels was visibly lost. *A Modern Instance*, unlike the earlier novels, begins with married life of Marcia and Bartley, their romance being cut short to the minimum and ends with the disintegration of marriage. The bleak pessimism which pervades the book was probably due to his personal trauma, which he underwent due to the illness of his eldest daughter and her eventual death. In *Indian Summer*, Howells tried to revive the spirit of his early fiction through his strategic retreat to the comic romance between aging man and a young woman. This novel is a love story which involves a young girl Imogene Graham with Theodore Colville who has just crossed forty, and in their misplaced love affair, Howells once again takes up the anti-sentimental stance which he had taken in many of his earlier novels as one of the side issues, but in this novel he has taken it as a major issue.

Adverse circumstances work in such a way that Theodore Colville comes to visit the same place where he was left heart-broken by a girl almost twenty years ago. After leaving his active commercial life at Das Vaches, Colville has returned to Florence, to search for lost youth, which eventually ends in a futile fiasco. Here, once again he meets Mrs. Bowen, who had been a friend and a confidant of his lost love. The tone of the novel is set, at the very beginning of the novel as the very first word 'midway' suggests the point of 'midway' in the span of Colville's life and the very opening sentence suggests the dilemma of right choice which Colville will have to face. "Midway of the Ponte Vecchio at Florence, where three arches break the lives of the little jewels booths glittering on either hand, and open an approach to parapet, Colville lounged against the corner of a shop and started out upon the river."[15]

Almost twenty years back, he had felt humiliated and defeated in love, by a young girl, Jenny Wheelwright, when he was a young architect in Florence. "She left him in possession of that treasure to a man of his temperament, a broken heart. From that time his vague dreams began to lift and to let him live in the clear light of common day" (*Summer*: 596). In the novel, much space is not devoted to his life in Das Vaches as a popular editor of Democrat Republican. We are just told that he is forced to snap ties with the paper and the place, when he has to face humiliating defeat when he is "flattered into running for Congress" (p.550). The defeat fills Colville's mind with 'disgust' as he cannot reconcile to the fact that he, who had been a name in Das Vaches, whose opinion was counted so much, as people of all parties had so much faith in him, could be defeated thus. "He stood disgraced before the community not only as a dangerous man and what was worse, he could not wholly acquit himself a measure of bad faith: his conscience troubled him even more than his pride" (p. 594). Through the deliberate use of irony, Howells shows that even the past bitter experiences have not been sufficient for Colville to lead a rational life in the "clear light of common day". Though this novel has been read as a light-hearted anti-sentimental comedy which lacks any deeper undertone except that of being an anti-romance, yet in a way it can also be read as a growth of Colville's realistic vision, who, in spite of being a middle-aged man, does not possess a clear view of life and that is why he succumbs to the charms of young Imogene Graham. In delineation of Colville's character, there is no stern moralist engaged in presenting a decaying civilization as in case of Bartley Hubbard in *A Modern Instance*. Yet the novel has a moral force which is beautifully woven in the narrative structure of the novel by Howells, whose unassuming integrity and commitment to the cause of truth and reality and rejection of romantic ideals and misconceptions never, in any novel, wavered. In this sense, Howells artistic affinity with Anton Chekov and George Eliot is noticeable.

In the relationship between Imogene Graham and Colville, it is not the disparity of their age alone, at which Howells laughs, it is Colville's weak and unsure disposition, like that of Don Ippolito and Miles Arbuton, that is the target of Howells' attack. Colville is fully aware that he is an aging man, already forty, and he knows that his youthful attraction for Imogene Graham is going to be disastrous for him. "Her abandon interested Colville, and then awed him, the spectacle of that young, unjaded capacity for pleasure touched him with a profound sense of loss" (p. 643). Again and again, Howells provides us with specific hints as to this "sense of loss" which Colville feels due to the difference in the age between him and

Imogene, "... he had his modest misgivings whether he were equal to quite so much young lady as Miss Graham seemed" (p.615). In spite of this lurking fear, Colville cannot resist the attraction because he feels "he had not yet lived his life, that his was a baffled destiny, an arrested fate" (p. 654).

At the age of Imogene Graham, to be romantic and sentimental is excusable, but at Colville's age, when he has freight of experience and a matured vision, it is unbelievable that he should go astray. As realistic romance is the controlling principle of the novel, the Italian background of the novel is functional, not merely decorative. "The Cascine Park and the Boboli Gardens which adorn it and the orchards and vineyards and cypress in the surrounding hills which frame it impart a sense of perpetual Garden World."[16] It is in this "perpetual garden world", that Colville tends to lose the sense of his age and in nostalgic urge for lost youth, mistakenly takes Imogene's immature infatuation as love. A perfect juxtaposition of Colville's lost world of beauty and youth with the scenic background of Florence is a technical achievement for which Howells has earned rightful praise from many critics.

In the course of the novel Colville reverts again and again to the illusions of youth in order to find common ground with Imogene and becomes more of an object of laughter. He tries to keep pace with her youthful activities of dancing and attending parties and realizes gradually that he is a misfit. In their first meeting, Imogene finds Colville's droll quite amusing and different from the usual immature manner of young man of her age. The way he talks of his past affair with Mrs. Bowen touches Imogene's sympathy and also wins her admiration, but at the same time she is not able to forget his age. "Yes, he's fascinating. But how old and sad he looked as he lay back there in the chair" (*Summer*: 628). Colville is also aware that he has made an impact on young Imogene and he is happy but at the same time unsure of himself.

> The looks of these two charming women followed him into his dreams, he knew he must have pleased them, and though it had been many years since he had found it sufficient cause of happiness to have pleased a woman, the desire to do so was by no means extinct in him. The eyes of the girl hovered above him like stars, he felt in their soft gaze that he was a romance to her young heart and this made him laugh, it also made him sigh (*Summer*: 629).

Tempting no doubt the opportunity is, because Imogene, in her youthful fancies undertakes to redeem Colville of the tragic past, of which Colville himself is not acutely aware. She starts imagining that "there's always an undercurrent of sadness---a tragedy---in everything for him" (p.637). Colville's attempts, at Madame Uccell's party to impress Imogene, by dancing in a stupid manner, produce a comic effect and many critics have found his manner and behaviour funny and foolish, which they think, does not behove of a respectable, well established and mature man of his age. But it is only fair to note that Colville's attempts to find a common ground with Imogene, no doubt appear foolish and obtuse, but they are in no way unrealistic. The intimacy which Colville develops with Bowens and Imogene Graham and the privileges that he starts enjoying with these ladies only provide him "with the futureless satisfaction of a man" (p. 682). In this respect, Gardner's comment that "If Colville's predicament had been the thematic centre of the novel, *Indian Summer* might have been Howells' masterpiece",[17] is correct to a certain extent. That would have definitely made the novel a great realistic comedy. But Howells, in that crucial decade, when he wrote *Indian Summer* was different from Howells of the earlier phase, when he concentrated more on love themes. Even the declared intention of Howells in this novel, was to dismantle the romantic citadel of self-sacrifice which Imogene constructs around Colville's personality. Her unrealistic sentimentality is not the butt of Howells' ridicule, it is an exposition of that code of popular fiction, which Colville is not able to live up to.

In the characters of Imogene Graham and Mrs. Bowen Howells has beautifully drawn the characteristics of the respective age to which they belong. There is a lot in Imogene's character that is in direct contrast to Mrs. Bowen's. If the former is an ingenue, impulsive, extrovert and young, the latter is a mature balanced lady who is an introvert. But in the power of their jealous outbursts both display the intensity which is similar, though Mrs. Bowen is able to hide hers in her quiet withdrawal and Imogene Graham becomes quite outspoken. Oscar W. Firkins' comment in this regard is noteworthy when he says: "Their characters are less attractive as individuals than as members of a select class."[18] While tracing the authenticity and superior vitality of the characters of Imogene Graham and Mrs. Bowen, Kenneth Eble feels, Howells has directly drawn the character of Imogene from his own daughter. He says: "Winny's presence and freshness of her responses to Italy" and his wife Elinor Mead furnished with Mrs. Bowen's character "particularly that New England rectitude that inclines toward both self-sacrifice and idealization of self."[19]

Mrs. Bowen's response to the relationship which develops between Colville and Imogene apart from being a reaction of secret lover, is "a successful dramatization of romantic-sentimental as against the realistic point of view."[20] Mrs. Bowen realizes from the beginning that the relationship between Colville and Imogene is based on bottomless, abstract romantic fancies which have no reality about them. Though Imogene is Mrs. Bowen's protegee, and she (Mrs. Bowen) has all rights to check her, she cannot forbid her to enter into this affair, because in her hearts of hearts, she is secretly in love with him. Miss Bowen's love for Colville is not at all like that of Imogene who "loves me (him) through her mistaken pity" (*Summer*: 799). In fact, the whole structure of the novel is built up on romanticist follies of not one, but three main characters—Imogene, Colville and Mrs. Bowen. After the engagement, Imogene realizes the folly of her misplaced choice in Colville, but the fear of betrayal does not let her muster enough courage to let Colville know of her fault. Colville, too is acutely aware of what mismatch Imogene and he are going to make, but once again, for the fear of breaking the young woman's heart, he keeps up the pretence of being happy with her. It is Mrs. Bowen's unrealistic notion of self-sacrifice that does not let Colville know of her true feelings for him. Out of the three, it is Mrs. Bowen who has the most practical approach to the subject of love and marriage and who has the typical Howellsian clear-sightedness to know that in her marriage with Colville, there is a lot of "adjustment of temperaments, the compromise of opinions, the reconciliation of tastes"[21] involved. Ultimately Colville and Imogene come face to face with the long-delayed reality. In the incident of the carriage accident at the end of the novel, Colville's instinctive reaction of saving Mrs. Bowen and Effie, instead of Imogene is enough reason for Imogene to break with him, but it relieves both Colville and Imogene. Cady has shown, through the evidence from the manuscript of *Indian Summer*, how the problem of ending worried Howells, who could not, at the end of the novel show that Colville takes such a risk of his life in saving Mrs. Bowen and Effie, because that would, once again, have brought into focus the sentimentalism, which Howells could not tolerate. Cady has furnished the evidence. "It must be Effie who brings C and Mrs. B together at last, with a burst of grief at C's going away."[22] The incorrigible realist that Howells was,

Colville's romantic impulse to save Mrs. Bowen, could not fit in with his scheme of realism and in the end it is for Effie's sake that both Colville and Mrs. Bowen decide to marry, not out of love. Even in the closing sentence of the novel when Mrs. Bowen, perforce, agrees to marry Colville and asks him to stay "in the self-contemptuous voice of a woman who falls below her ideal of herself" (*Summer*: 855), Howells' implicit irony is at work.

Even Mrs. Bowen has set certain ideals, which, Howells shows in the novel, are impractical and false. By the time he wrote *Indian Summer*, his approach towards youth, romance and love had changed. Though apparently, Imogene Graham seems to belong to the tradition of Kitty Ellisons and Lydia Bloods, there is a remarkable difference in Howells' own approach to this young heroine who does not behave with the spontaneity that had contributed so much to the grace of Kitty and Lydia, as she behaves with some unnatural constraint and inhibition to fulfill her role as a heroine.

Despite the elements of romance in the three novels discussed in this chapter---the semi-tragic legend in *A Chance Acquaintance*, the tragi-comic ending in *A Foregone Conclusion* and the comic irony of *Indian Summer*---they are all concerned with the realities of man's life in a society full of social disparities. They all concern themselves with the process by which the distorted ideals either lead to the defeat of the individual in society, like that of Don Ippolito in *A Foregone Conclusion* or are modified and chastened in him by disillusion and social education like Kitty Ellison in *A Chance Acquaintance*.

The common psychological burden under which the struggling characters in Howells' novels labor, contrary to the usual expectations of American reading public of the time unravel the issues of real importance. In the success and failure of Silas Lapham, Lemuel Barker, Jeff Durgin, Bartley Hubbard and many others, Howells perceived that the fundamental reality of modern American life was its impermanence. Although he has dealt with the serious consequences of this condition with a charmingly deceptive humor, yet there are moments when he is unable to hide his narrator's sense of uneasiness, at the sheer lack of moral standards.

Notes

1. John W. Crowley, "An Interoceanic Episode: *The Lady of the Aroostook*" in *On Howells: The Best from American Literature*, Edwin H. Cady and Louis J. Budd. (Durham: Duke University Press, 1993): 259.
2. Darel Abel, *American Literature 3 Vols.* (New York: Baroom's Educational Series, 1963): 3:143.
3. William Dean Howells: *A Chance Acquaintance* (Bloomington: Indiana University Press, 1971): 91. Subsequent references to this edition will be abbreviated as *Chance*.
4. John W. Crowley, *The Black Heart's Truth: The Early Career of W.D. Howells* (Chapel Hill: University of North Carolina Press, 1985): 73.
5. William McMurray, *The Literary Realism of William Dean Howells* (Carbondale: Southern Illinois University Press, 1967): 5.
6. W.D. Howells, *A Foregone Conclusion*, *Howells' Novels, 1875-1886* (New York: Literary Classics of the United States, 1982): Subsequent references to this edition will be abbreviated as *Conclusion*.
7. Olov W. Fryckste, *In Quest of America: A Study of Howells' Early Development as a Novelist* (Cambridge: Harvard University Press, 1958): 152.

8. Richard, Foster, "The Contemporaneity of Howells", *New England Quarterly*, 32 (1959): 57.
9. Alfred Habegger, *Gender, Fantasy and Realism in American Literature* (New York: Columbia University Press, 1982): 244.
10. Henry James, Qtd. in Ellen F. Wright: William Dean Howells and the Irrational *Nineteenth Century Fiction*, 38 (1983-84): 312.
11. Amy Kaplan, *The Social Construction of American Realism* (Chicago: University of Chicago Press, 1988): 58.
12. George Arms, "The Literary Background of Howells' Social Criticism" *On Howells: The Best from American Literature*, Edwin H. Cady and Louis J. Budd (Durham: Duke University Press, 1993): 7.
13. Kenneth E. Eble, *William Dean Howells*, 2nd ed. (Boston: Twayne, 1982): 1.
14. Charles L. Campbell, "Realism and Romance of Real life, Multiple Fictional Worlds in Howells' Novels", *Modern Fiction Studies* 16 (1970): 290.
15. W.D. Howells, *Indian Summer* in *Howells' Novels, 1875-1886.* (New York: Literary Classics of the United States, 1982): I. Subsequent reference to this edition will be abbreviated as *Summer*.
16. Elsa Nettles, *Language Race and Social Class in Howells' America* (Lexington: University of Kentucky Press, 1987): 132.
17. Joseph H. Gardner, "Howells: The Realist as Dickensian", *Modern Fiction Studies*, 16 (3) 1970:325.
18. Oscar W. Firkins, *William Dean Howells: A Study* (Cambridge: Harvard University Press, 1924): 123.
19. Eble, 85.
20. William Dean Howells, *The Day of Their Wedding Journey* (New York: Harper, 1896): 86-87.
21. Cady, *Road*: 228.
22. Cady, *Road*: 226.

7

Conclusion

That realism is out-moded and the realistic novel has lost its literary function, is a commonplace criticism sufficiently widespread to be familiar to even those who only even casually associated with literature. The critical opinion these days subscribes to the view that in the current literary scene, there is no chance for realism to grow. In fact, the hostility to realism and realistic fiction is so strong that if by chance a writer continues to write in realistic tradition he is compared to "headless chickens unaware of the decapitating axe."[1] The argument for abandoning reality and realism follows from the basic premise that "reality is no longer realistic."[2] It is quite surprising that collapse of confidence in realism occurred in France from where this movement is supposed to have emerged. In France it fell into sudden disrepute primarily because realism there had already degenerated into naturalism. Naturalism as a movement became defunct due to its obsessive attention to the more seamy aspects of life.

Due to the change of ideology after World War I, many

writers who dominated the literary scene during the later half of the nineteenth century were eliminated from the American literary canon. Why, with the turn of the century, authors like Benjamin Franklin, Washington Irving, James Fenimore Cooper, William Cullen Bryant, James Russell Lowell, Henry Wadsworth Longfellow, Oliver Wendell Holmes, Sidney, Lanier and William Dean Howells got devalued and at the same time, why those like Twain and James got elevated is a matter which has limitless arguments for and against the situation.

Apart from general reaction against rationalism and dispassionate, objective portrayal of reality, the causes of the decline of realism also lay in the lack of confidence in the future of middle class. F.W.J. Hemmings' remark on this aspect is pertinent to note when he says:

> ....the middle class public grew increasingly averse to reading harrowing accounts of the 'seamy side' of life in slums, factories and impoverished villages. Instead, it looked to its writers to provide an imaginary refuge from reality, it applauded any and every experiment in escaping, from reality, from historicism to occultism from any symbolism to the grossest forms of decadent eroticism.[3]

The problem lay not with the sudden distaste for the material of the writers of the realistic fiction, but with the changing times and the scenario, the rapidity of which these authors could not catch up. In fact, the realism that developed in American fiction in the 1880s and 1890s is an anxious mode, which both articulates and combats this growing sense of unreality at the heart of middle-class life. A realist found it more and more difficult to capture the growing sense of unreality.

The post-World War II American literature relegated the

realistic novel into the background, as bipolar approach to prose narratives started regarding fact and fiction as two antithetical poles. John Fowles' confession right in the middle of his novel *The French Lieutenant's Women* is the open rejection of even the illusion of reality: "The story I am telling is all imagination. These characters I create never existed outside my own mind."[4]

The decline of the realistic period has its roots in the literary revaluation that became rigidified as the linear nature of reality started being questioned more and more. Perhaps, this strong sense of unreality was due to a widespread belief that twentieth century reality is 'unreal' and that it is therefore "unsuitable for realistic treatment."[5] So it is in the very nature of contemporary reality, that it makes it no longer amenable to realistic treatment. In Graff's assessment, "the rhetoric of recent criticism have tended either to overlook this reality-centered aspect or to delay its existence---on the grounds that reality cannot be understood at all or that understanding it objectively is the special job of some other discipline."[6]

The interrelationship between literary ideology and social intellectual scenario is too complicated for simple formulation. Realism as a genre, suffered a setback due to the emergence of modern technological reality, which in some profound sense appeared unreal, and made many writers and critics leap to the conclusion that literature must for this reason abandon its pretensions to represent external reality. The imposition of strict conventions on this literary genre proved suffocating for its survival. Too much insistence on exact and objective reproduction of real life and an absolute reverence for the material surface of things with detached observation made realism more of a critical theory and less of creative enterprise. Realism, actually, had no way out other than to flop in the current situation. It could fully bloom and flourish during the last decades of nineteenth century and the earliest decade of the twentieth century when fragmentation caused due to the emergence of industrial society had not encroached upon individual lives. The mental and intellectual vacuum created after the World Wars could not be filled by mere realistic details. The tortured and injured human psyche, after facing the trauma of the wars, required a balm which realism could not offer. Creative writing, then, reverted back to romantic genre as it expressed faith, "in the constitutive power of the imagination a confidence in the ability of literature to impose order, value, and meaning on the chaos and fragmentation of industrial society. Literature increasingly adopted an ironic view of its traditional pretensions to truth, high seriousness, and the profundity of 'meaning'."[7]

As Lionel Trilling says, "we are not easy with the quiet men, the civil personalities."[8] So the demands of the reading public changed. There was a gradual decline in realism as a genre during the early years of twentieth century, in spite of the fact that it appeared prominently in the nation's leading publications like *Century*, *Harpers* and *North American Review*. Its reiterated insistence on truthful art and highlighted its lack of artifice. The obsession with merely tangible and concrete truth made them overlook the fact that there also existed a deeper, eternal truth, not necessarily perceivable and measurable. In his introduction to *American Realism*, Sundquist contends that American realism "did not achieve a certain and stable force, exhaust that force and perish, rather it failed case by case by refusing to renounce romance completely and by leveling the barriers of aesthetic freedom too completely."[9]

Although realists were the first group of American authors

to consciously work out a full body of theory about the purpose, function and quality of literature, they violated their theoretical premises as often as they observed them (though Howells is an exception to this observation because except very rarely, he rigidly stuck to his realistic theory). Fidelity to everyday life and to probability of motive were easier to theorize about than to realize. The classic texts of American realism do not wholly lack intruding narrators, coincidences, improbabilities and exaggerated moments of life, deployed as plot devices. In addition to these textual qualities often associated with romanticism, realism, as Borus observed, "also pointed ahead to modernism with the use of subjective narration, a stress on the fragmented self, and forays into symbolism and impressionism, all of which contradicted the realist dictum of anchored reality."[10]

Why did the self-conscious movement of realism fizzle out? From the point of view of the post-structuralist theories the stance taken by the realists of the objective representation of reality became an impossibility. The post-structuralists believed that the chasm between the subject and the object is too much for the survival of straight-forward realism. In fact, it is this blatant acceptance of the subject-object dichotomy on which the modernist postulates are based. Working against the illusory nature of reality, modernism rejected the ideals of objectivity and inclusiveness upon which realism imagined itself to be based. Robert Alter's comment on death of modernism applied equally to realism when he says "the high tide of realism too ebbed. Just as realism started as an openly declared revolt against sentimental romance, modernism became the self-conscious overturning of the convention of bourgeois realism."[11]

It is perfectly understandable that the birth of any

self-conscious or otherwise literary movement is just a matter of rise and fall of shared impulse and mostly it has to do with the desire for a reversal and change. May be due to saturation or exhaustion, a new movement appears, phoenix-like, suddenly catching the fancy of majority of literary minds. That doesn't mean that the previous movement should be considered merely as an aberration and thus repudiated. Now, when the modernist and post-modernist stance taken by the critics has finally rejected the plausibility of Howells and his brand of realism, it does not mean that we should close our eyes to his contribution in saving American literature from artificiality that threatened to engulf it in a tide of historical romances and sentimental novels.

The rise of implausible themes in literature and growing interest in fabulous myths of science fiction and also the dominance of the dream worlds and anti-worlds does not necessarily mean that realism is out of the literary scene. Hostility to realistic fiction, in part arises from widespread critical position that realism should give way to fantasy or to self-referential meta-fiction.

Any attempt at appraisal of Howells' place in American literature, has also, perforce, to take into account the factors responsible for gradual extinction of realism, because Howells and realism cannot be studied in isolation. The factors responsible for the rise and fall of realism run almost parallel to Howells' position in American literature. The reasons which caused the gradual decline of realism had the most detrimental impact on Howells' reputation. Born and raised in the social, physical and intellectual climate of pre-industrial America, it was a painful process for Howells to come to terms with the industrializing America. The writers engaged in creative writings between 1890 and the end of World War I found themselves inextricably caught in the struggle between traditional dogmas and scientific and industrialized world. In *The Hazard of New Fortunes*, Howells has beautifully captured this struggle, as the claims of the shadowy urban working class continually threatened to explode middle-class community. So the opinion held by several critics that Howells lacked the ability to portray those classes outside his immediate purview, is misplaced. The prime factor responsible for the decline in his reputation has been the erroneous notion that Howells dealt with the smiling aspects alone in his fiction. The entire argument of my study has pointed to the contrary. Even in his earliest fumbling as a writer he has shown his interest in the 'unsmiling' aspects of American life. In his early novels like *Their Wedding Journey*, *A Foregone Conclusion* and *A Chance Acquaintance*, which have generally been read as comedy of manners and as being based on courtship themes, the dark ironic undertone has been traced which is so implicit that to a casual reader it is not apparent. In the novels exploring marriage and love as the main theme, Howells did not satisfy the popular romantic sentiment as he did not idealize any of his heroes or heroines. In fact, many of his novels were written by him specifically with the purpose of proving false many unrealistic notions. In doing so, he had to give sudden twist to his endings, whenever he sensed the danger of his novel lapsing into a tragedy or a romance.

Howells' bellicose argument for realism, rendered forceful due to his influential association with *Atlantic Monthly* as its editor and then as a critic for *Harper's Monthly* has persisted till now, despite all the efforts against it by his detractors. In his critical outpourings Howells tried to operate on two levels, firstly, by taking the offensive against the outmoded literary conventions and secondly as a defense for newer and more threatening alternatives. Due to this dual perspective, Howells gave rise to larger number of detractors than usual. As Amy Kaplan puts it, "despite the vehemence with which Howells launched his attacks, the opponents of realism remained elusive and hydra-headed as the concept of realism itself."[12]

The most important factor that contributed to the sudden disappearance of Howells was that his creative genius got suffocated in the claustrophobic limitations of his realistic theory. Deep inside, Howells himself was aware of the ultimate unrealistic nature of reality. Comparing himself to an onion he says that it is "nothing but hulls, that you keep peeling off, one after another, till you think you have got down to the heart at last and then you have got down to nothing."[13]

What an irony that out of the three major realists of the late nineteenth century---Mark Twain, Henry James and William Dean Howells---it is Howells who is supposed to be the pioneer in initiating a trend and who has suffered most. To quote Jerry Herron, "if he'd been a more cynical man, he might have become a trickster like his friend Mark Twain, or if he'd learned to believe in form instead of yearning for the lost presence of God, he might have become Henry James. But he was neither, which makes him finally better company than both. Not a better read, necessarily, but a more accommodating text."[14]

As a perceptive realist, Howells could foresee the short-lived span of realism as he declared:

> When realism becomes false to itself, when it heaps up facts merely, and maps life instead of picturing it, realism will perish....Every true realist instinctively knows this, and it is perhaps the reason why he is careful of every fact, and feels himself bound to express or to indicate its meaning at the risk of over moralising.[15]

Such a position as Howells fixes for a realist, was bound to be eroded in post-World War era as Sarah B. Daugherty suggests that such "logocentric position" as held by Howells was "rejected by the post-modernists, who deny the existence of any intrinsic "truth or meaning".[16]

Contemporary critics are no longer much agitated over the threat of realistic fiction to American morals nor over its inattention to the ideal conception generally discussed as an historical phenomenon of techniques by which an artist sought to achieve particular effects of verisimilitude. In his recent reassessment, Howells has been granted the validity of his artistic aims and theories, and if some critics direct their critical attention to the degree of his success others also point out his faults. Their assumption is that they are dealing with a conscious and accomplished artist, and their aim is to discover and explain how Howells' artistry works.

Though Howells fails the modernist test of literary greatness and his realistic imagination is antithetical to modernist sensibility, one is reminded of Trilling's remark in this context: "When we are so eager to say how wrong Howells was to invite the novelist to deal with the smiling aspects of life, we have to ask ourselves whether our quick antagonism to this mild recognition of pleasure does not imply an impatience with the self---a degree of yielding to what Hannah Arendt calls 'the irresistible temptation of disintegration'."[17]

The more important issue is not whether realism fails or succeeds, but how realism works to construct a social world out of the raw materials of unreality, conflict and change. And that Howells has been successful in constructing a homogeneous and coherent social reality, by conquering the fictional qualities of middle-class life and by controlling the spectre of class conflict, is obvious in the analysis of his works, undertaken in this book.

To sum up the whole argument, there is no doubt that sincere efforts have been undertaken by recent critics for the re-interpretation of Howells' achievement as a novelist. Though his place in the literary history of America is secure, a time will come when this almost forgotten novelist of the past will receive the attention which is his due share.

Notes

1. Robert Scholes, *The Fabulators* (New York: Oxford University Press, 1967): 6.
2. Norman Mailer, Qtd. by Raymond Tallia, *In Defense of Realism*, (London: Arnold, 1988): 8.
3. F.W.J. Hemmings, ed., *The Age of Realism* (Sussex: The Harvester Press, 1978): 361.
4. Brian Machle, *Post-Modernist Fiction* (London: Routledge, 1989): 197.
5. Tallis: 9.
6. Gerald Graff, *Literature Against Itself. Literary Ideas in Modern Society* (Chicago: University of Chicago Press, 1979).
7. Graff, op. cit: 33.
8. Lionel Trilling, "W.D. Howells and the Roots of Modern Tastes", *Opposing Self Nine Essays in Criticism* (New York: Viking Press, 1955): 82.
9. Eric Sundquist, *American Realism: New Essays* (Baltimore: John Hopkins University Press, 1982): 9.
10. Daniel Borus, *Writing Realism: Howells, James and Norris in the Mass Market* (Chapel Hill: University of North Carolina Press, 1989): 117.

11. Robert Alter, Qtd in Joha Barth, "The Literature of Replenishment" *Artlantic Monthly* (Jan, 1980): 67.
12. Amy Kaplan, *Social Construction of American Realism* (Chicago: University of Chicago Press, 1988): 15.
13. W.D. Howells, *A Boy's Town* (New York: Harpers and Brothers, 1980): 171.
14. Jerry Herron, "Howells on My Mind: Reflections on Deans, Sesquicentennial", *New England Quarterly*, 61 (1988): 199.
15. Edwin H. Cady ed., *W.D. Howells as a Critic* (London: Routledge and Kegan Paul, 1973): 136.
16. Sarah B. Daugherty, "Howells, Tolstoy and the Limits of Realism: The Case of Annie Kilburn" *American Literary Realism* 19 (1987): 22.
17. Trilling, 102.

Bibliography

Primary Sources

Books

Howells, William Dean, *The Altrurian Romances*, Bloomington: Indiana University Press, 1968.

—, *Annie Kilburn: A Novel*, Upper Saddle River, N.J.: Literature House/Gregg Press, 1970.

—, *April Hopes*, Bloomington: Indiana University Press, 1974.

—, *Between the Dark and Daylight Romances*, New York: Harper and Row, 1970.

—, *A Chance Acquaintance*, Bloomington: Indiana University Press, 1971.

—, *The Coast of Bohemia*, New York: Harper and Row, 1890.

—, *A Foregone Conclusion* in *Howells Novels 1875-1886*. New York: Literary Classics of the United States, 1982.

—, *Hazard of New Fortunes*, New York: New American Library, 1967.

—, *Imaginary Interviews*, New York: Greenwood Press, 1969.

—, *Indian Summer: Howells Novels 1875-1886*, New York: Literary Classics of the United States, 1982.

—, *Italian Journeys*, Boston: Houghton, 1895.

—, *The Kentons*, Bloomington: Indiana University Press, 1971.

—, *The Lady of the Aroostook*, Boston: Houghton, 1879.

—, *The Landlord at Lion's Head*, New York: The New American Library, 1964.

—, *The Leatherwood God*, New York: Century, 1916.

—, *Literature and Life*, Studies, Port Washington, N.Y.: Kennikat Press, 1968.

—, *Literary Friends and Acquaintances: A Personal Retrospect of American Authorship*, Bloomington: Indiana University Press, 1968.

—, *Main-travelled Roads*, New York: Harper and Row, 1956.

—, *The Minister's Charge*, St. Clair Stores, Michigan: Scholarly Press, 1887.

—, *Miss Bellard's Inspiration*, New York: Harper and Row, 1905.

—, *A Modern Instance*, New York: New American Library, 1964.

—, *Modern Italian Poets: Essays and Versions*, With Portraits, New York: Harper and Row, 1887.

—, *My Literary Passions*, New York: Harper, 1910.

—, *The Quality of Mercy*, St. Clair Stores, Michigan: Scholarly Press, 1968.

—, *Questionable Shapes*, New York: Harper and Row, 1903.

—, *Ragged Lady*, New York: Harper and Row, 1899.

—, *The Rise of Silas Lapham*, New York: Rinehart, 1949.

—, *The Shadow of a Dream*, and An Imperative Duty, Bloomington: Indiana University Press, 1970.

—, *The Son of Royal Langbirth*, Bloomington: Indiana University Press, 1969.

—, *The Story of Play*, New York: Harper and Row, 1898.

—, *Their Silver Wedding Journey*, New York: Harper and Row, 1899.

---, *Their Wedding Journey*, Boston: Osgood, 1872.

---, *The Undiscovered Country*, Boston: Houghton, 1880.

---, *Venetian Life*, Cambridge: Riverside Press, 1907.

---, *Years of My Youth*, New York: Harper and Row, 1916.

Collections of Writings by Howells Under Other Auspices

The Complete Plays of W.D. Howells, ed. Walter J. Meserve, New York: New York University Press, 1960.

Criticism and Fiction and Other Essays, ed. Clara M. and Rudolf Kirk, New York: New York University Press, 1960.

Discovery of a Genious: William Dean Howells and Henry James, ed. Albert Mordell, New York: Twayne, 1961.

Editor's Study by William Dean Howells, ed. James W. Simpson, Troy, N.Y.: Whitson, 1983.

If Not Literature, ed. Ginette de B. Merrill and George Arms, Columbus: Ohio State University Press, 1988.

Interviews with William Dean Howells, ed. Ulrich Halfmann, Arlington: American Literary Realism, 1973.

John Hay-Howells Letters: The Correspondence of John Milton Hay and William Dean Howells 1861-1905, ed. George Monteiro and Brenda Murphy, Boston: Turayne, 1980.

Life in Letters of William Dean Howells, ed. Mildred Howells, Garden City: Doubleday, 1928, Two Volumes.

Mark Twain-Howells Letters: The Correspondence of Mark Twain and William D. Howells 1872-1900, ed. Herry Nash Smith and William M. Gibson Cambridge: Harvard University Press, 1960, Two Volumes.

Prefaces of Contemporaries (1882-1920), ed. George Arms et al. Galnesville: Scholar's Facsimiles and Reprints, 1957.

W.D. Howells as Critic, ed. Edwin H. Cady, London: Routledge, 1973.

William Dean Howells: Representative Selections, with Introduction, Bibliography, and Notes (1920), ed. Clara M. and Rudolf Kirk. Rev. ed., New York: Hill and Wang, 1961.

Critical Writings on W.D. Howells

Alexander, William, *William Dean Howells: The Realist as Humanist*, New York: Burt Franklin, 1981.

Baker, William D., *William Dean Howells: The Influence of Ohio on His Life and Works*, Columbus: State Library of Ohio, 1979.

Bassett, John Earl, *A Heart of Ideality in My Realism and Other Essays on Howells and Twain*, West Cornwell: Locust Hill Press, 1991.

Bennett, George N., *The Realism of William Dean Howells, 1889-1920*, Nashville: Vanderbilt University Press, 1973.

---, *William Dean Howells: The Development of a Novelist*, Norman: University of Oklahoma Press, 1959.

Borus, Daniel, *Writing Realism Howells, James and Norris in the Mass Market*, Chapel Hill: University of North Carolina Press, 1989.

Brooks Van, Wyck, *Howells: His Life and World*, London: J.M. Dent, 1959.

Cady, Edwin H. Budd, Louis J., *On Howells: The Best from American Literature*, Durham: Duke University Press, 1993.

Cady, Edwin H., *The Realist at War: The Mature Years 1885-1920 of William Dean Howells*, Syracuse: Syracuse University Press, 1958.

---, *The Road to Realism: The Early Years 1837-1885 of William Dean Howells*, Syracuse: Syracuse University Press, 1996.

--- and Frazier, David L. (eds.), *The War of the Critics over William Dean Howells*, Evenston Ill: Row, Peterson, 1962.

Cady, Edwin H., *W.D. Howells, Dean of American Letters*, Syracuse, Syracuse University Press, 1956-58.

Cady, Edwin and Norma W. Cady, eds., *Critical Essays on W.D. Howells, 1866-1920*, Boston: Hall, 1983.

Carrington, George C. Jr., *The Immense Complex Drama: The World and Art of the Howells Novels*, Columbus: Ohio State University Press, 1966.

Carter, Everett, *Howells and the Age of Realism*, Philadelphia: Lippincott, 1954.

Crowley, John W., *The Black Heart's Truth: The Early Car[illegible] of W.D. Howells*, Chapel Hill: University of North Carolina Press, 1985.

Crowley, John W., *The Mask of Fiction: Essays on W.D.H.*, Amherst: University of Massachusetts Press, 1989.

Dean, James L., *Howells' Travels Toward Art*, Albuquerque University of New Mexico Press, 1970.

Eakin, Paul John, *The New England Girl: Cultural Ideals in Hawthorne, Stowe, Howells and James*, Athens: University of Georgia Press, 1976.

Eble, Kenneth E., ed., *Howells: A Century of Criticism*, Dallas: Southern Methodist University Press, 1962.

Eble, Kenneth E., *William Dean Howells*, 2nd ed., Boston: Twayne, 1982.

Eschholz, Paul A., ed., *Critics on William Dean Howells*, Coral Gables: University of Miami Press, 1975.

Firkins, Oscar W., *William Dean Howells: A Study*, Cambridge: Harvard University Press, 1924.

Frederick, John T., "William Dean Howells", *The Darkened Sky: Nineteenth Century American Novelists and Religion*, Notre Dame: University of Notre Dame Press, 1969.

Fryckste Olov W., *In Quest of America: A Study of Howells' Early Development as a Novelist*, Cambridge: Harvard University Press, 1958.

Gibson, William M., *Theodore Roosevelt Among the Humorists*, W.D. Howells, Mark Twain, and Mr. Dooley, Knoxville: University of Tennessee Press, 1980.

Gibson, William M., *William Dean Howells*, University of Minnesota Pamphlets on American Writers: Minneapolis, 1976.

Harvey, Alexander, *William Dean Howells: A Study of the Achievement of Literary Artist*, New York: B.W. Husbsch, 1971.

Hough, Robert L., *The Quiet Rebel: William Dean Howells as a Social Commentator*, Lincoln: University of Nebraska Press, 1959.

Kirk, Clara M., *W.D. Howells and Art in His Time*, New Brunswick: Rutgers University Press, 1965.

Kirk, Clara M. and Kirk, Rudolf, *William Dean Howells*, New York: Twayne, 1961.

Lynn, Kenneth S., *William Dean Howells: An American Life*, New York: Harcourt, 1971.

McMurray, William, *The Literary Realism of William Dean Howells*, Carbondale: Southern Illinois University Press, 1967.

Nettles, Elsa, *Language, Race and Social Class in Howells' America*, Lexington: University of Kentucky Press, 1987.

Olsen, Rodney D., *Dancing in Chains: The Youth of William Dean Howells*, New York: New York University Press, 1991.

Prioleau, Elizabeth S., *The Circle of Eros: Sexuality in the Works of William Dean Howells*, Durham: Duke University Press, 1983.

Taylor, Walter F., *The Economic Novel in American*, Chapel Hill: University of North Carolina Press, 1942.

Vanderbilt, Kermit, *The Achievement of William Dean Howells: A Reinterpretation*, Princeton: Princeton University Press, 1968.

Vanderbilt, Kermit, *William Dean Howells: The Friendly Eye*, New York: Oxford University Press, 1969.

Woodress, James L., *Howells and Italy*, Durham: Duke University Press, 1952.

Articles

Arms, George, "Howells' English Travel Books: Problems in Technique", *PMLA*, 82 (1967): 104-16.

---, "Howells' Last Travel Book", *The Old Northwest*, 8 (1982) 131-55.

----, "The Literary Background of Howells' Social Criticism", *American Literature*, 14 (1942): 260-76.

----, "Some Varieties of Howells' Religious Experience", *The American Self: Myth, Ideology and Popular Culture*, ed. Sam B. Girgus, Albuquerque: University of New Mexico Press, pp.76-87.

Baker, William O., "Howells: The Heritage of Eureka Mills", *Old Northwest*, 9 (1983): 255-65.

Baxter, Annette K., "Caste and Class: Howells' Boston and Whartons' New York", *Midwest Quarterly*, 4 (1963): 353-61.

Berces, Frances A. "Mimesis, Morality and The Rise of Silas Lapham", *American Quarterly*, 22 (1970): 190-202.

Bell, Michael D., "The Sin of Art and the Problem of American Realism: William Dean Howells", *Prospects*, 9 (1984): 115-42.

Beardman, Authur, "Social Point of View in the Novels of William Dean Howells", *American Literature*, 39 (March, 1967): 42-59.

Bremer, Sidney H., "Invalids and Actresses: Howells' Duplex Imagery for American Women", *American Literature*, 47 (1976): 599-614.

----, "William Dean Howells' Ingenues and the Road to Marriage", *American Literary Realism*, 12 (1979): 143-50.

Brenda, Murphy, "Howells and the Popular Story Paradigm: Reading Silas Lapham's Proairetic Code", *American Literary Realism*, 21 (Winter 1989): 25-40.

Brodhead, Richard H., "Howells: Literary History and the Realist Vocation", *The School of Hawthorne*, New York: Oxford University Press, 1986: pp.81-103.

Budd Louis J., "W.D. Howells' Defense of the Romance", *PMLA*, 67 (1952): 32-42.

----, "Twain, Howells and the Boston Nihilists", *New England Quarterly*, 32 (1959): 351-71.

----, Cady, Edwin H., "The Neuroticism of William Dean Howells", *PMLA*, 61 (1946): 22-38.

----, "A Note on Howells and The Smiling Aspects of Life", *American Literature*, 58 (1945): 175-78.

Campbell, Charles L., "Realism and the Romance of Real Life: Multiple Fictional Worlds in Howells' Novels", *Modern Fiction Studies*, 16 (1970): 289-302.

Carrington, George C. Jr., "Howells and the Dramatic Essay", *American Literary Realism*, 17 (1984): 44-46.

----, "Howells: The Aging Artist in the Easy Chair", *Old Northwest*, 8 (1982): 151-88.

Cook, Don L., "Realism and the Dangers of Parody", in W.D. Howells' Fiction *Old Northwest*, 8 (1982): 69-80.

Cowie, Alexander, "William Dean Howells", *The Rise of the American Novel*, New York: American Book, 1946: 653-701.

Crider, Gregory L. "William Dean Howells and the Antiurban Tradition: A Reconsideration", *American Studies*, 19, No. 1 (1978): 55-64.

Cronkhite, G. Ferris, "Howells Turns to the Inner Life", *New England Quarterly*, 30 (1957): 474-85.

Crowley, John W., "An Interoceanic Episode: The Lady of the Aroostook", *American Literature*, 49 (1977): 181-91.

Crowley, John W., "Howellsian Realism: A Psychological Juggle", *Studies in Literary Imagination*, 16, No. 2 (1983): 45-55.

----, "Howells, Stoddard, and the Illustrations for Summer Cruising in the South Seas", *Gay Studies Newsletter*, 13 (November, 1986): 23-25.

----, "Winifred Howells and the Economy of Pain", *Old Northwest*, 10 (1984); 41-75.

Cumpiano, Marion W., "The Dark Side of Their Wedding Journey", *American Literature*, 40 (1969): 472-86.

Cumpiano, Marion W., "Howells Bridge: A Study of the Artistry of Indian Summer", *Modern Fiction Studies*, 16 (1970): 363-81.

Daugherty, Sarah B., "Howells Reviews James: The Transcendence of Realism", *American Literary Realism*, 18 (1985): 147-64.

----, "Howells, Tolstoy and the Limits of Realism: The Case of Annie Kilburn", *American Literary Realism*, 19 (1987): 21-30.

Delbanco, Andrew, "Howells and the Suppression of Knowledge", *Southern Review*, 19 (1983): 765-84.

DuPree, Ellen Philips, "Wharton, Lewis and the Nobel Prize Address", *American Literature*, 56 (1984): 262-70.

Eby, Clara Virginia, "Compromise and Complicity in The Rise of Silas Lapham", *American Literary Realism*, 24 (1991): 39-53.

Edel, Leon, "A Suburban Friendship", *Henry James: The Untired Years*, Philadelphia: Lippincott, 1953: 268-76.

Erickson, C.A., "The Tough and Tender-Minded: W.D. Howells' *The Landlord at Lion's Head*", *Studies in the Novel*, 17 (1985); 383-94.

Ewell, Barbara C., "Paradic Echoes of *The Portrait of a Lady* in Howells' *Indian Summer*", *Tulana Studies in English*, 22 (1977): 117-31.

Fischer, William C. Jr., "William Dean Howells: Reverie and the Nonsymbolic Aesthetic", *Nineteenth Century Fiction*, 25 (1970): 1-30.

Foster, Richard, "The Contemporaneity of Howells", *New England Quarterly*, 32 (1959): 54-78.

Fox, Arnold B., "Howells as a Religious Critic", *New England Quarterly*, 25 (1952): 199-216.

Frazier, David L., "Their Wedding Journey: Howells' Fictional Craft", *New England Quarterly*, 42 (1969): 323-49.

----, "Time and the Theme of Indian Summer", *Arizona Quarterly*, 36 (1960): 260-67.

Gardner, Joseph H., "Howells: The 'Realist' as Dickensian", *Modern Fiction Studies*, 16 (1970): 323-43.

Gibson, William M., "Mark Twain and Howells: Anti-Imperialists", *New England Quarterly*, 20 (1947): 435-70.

----, "Materials and Form in Howells' First Novels", *American Literature*, 19 (1947): 158-66.

Gibson, William M., "W.D. Howells and 'The Ridiculous Human Heart", *Studies in American Humor*, 2 (1975): 32-45.

Gifford, Henry, "W.D. Howells: His Moral Conservatism", *Kenyon Review*, 20 (1958): 124-33.

Girgus, Sam B., "Howells and Marcuse: A Forecast of the One-Dimensional Age", *American Quarterly*, 25 (1973): 108-18.

----, "The New Age of Narcissism: The Sexual Politics of Howells' A Modern Instance", *Mosaic*, 19 (1986): 33-44.

Green, Martin, "Marriage in Howells and Lawrence", *Transatlantic Patterns: Cultural Comparisons of England with America*, New York: Basic Books, 1977: 7-17.

Gross, Seymour, and Rosalie Murphy, "Commonplace Reality and the Romantic Phantoms: Howells' A Modern Instance and the Rise of Silas Lapham", *Studies in American Fiction*, 4 (1976): 1-14.

Habegger, Alfred, "The Autistic Tyrant, Howells' Self-Sacrificial Woman and Jamesian Renunciation", *Novel*, 10 (1976): 27-39.

----, "Nineteenth Century American Humor: Easy-going Males, Anxious Ladies and Penelope Lapham", *PMLA*, 91 (1976): 884-97.

----, "W.D. Howells and the 'American Girl'", *Taxes Quarterly*, 19 (1976) 149-56.

Hart, John E., "The Commonplace as Heroic in The Rise of Silas Lapham", *Modern Fiction Studies*, 8 (1992-1963): 375-83.

Hedges, Elaine R., "Ce'sal Birotteau and The Rise of Silas Lapham: A Study in Parallels", *Nineteenth Century Fiction*, 17 (1962): 163-74.

Herron, Jerry, "Howells on My Mind: Reflections on Dean's Sesquicentennial", *New England Quarterly*, 61 (1988): 183-200.

Hirsch, David, "William Dean Howells and Daisy Miller", *English Language Notes*, I (1963): 123-28.

Hoffman, Frederick J., "Henry James, William Dean Howells, and the Art of Fiction", *The Modern Novel in America*, Chicago: Regnery, 1951.

Jackson, Fleda B., "The Search for Sermons in Stones: The Pastoral Journey in A Modern Instance", *Colby Library Quarterly*, 21 (1985): 34-44.

Jackson, Fleda Brown, "A Sermon without Exegesis: The Achievement of Stasis in The Rise of Silas Lapham", *Journal of Narrative Technique*, 16 (1986): 131-47.

Jacobson, Marcia, "The Mask of Fiction: William Dean Howells' Experiments in Autobiography", *Biography*, 10 (1987): 55-67.

Jones, Joel M., "A Shaker Village Revisited: The Familial Ideal in the World of William Dean Howells", *Old Northwest*, 8 (1982): 82-100.

Kaplan, Amy, "The Knowledge of the Line: Realism and City in Howells' A Hazard of New Fortunes", *PMLA*, 101 (1986): 69-81.

Kar, Annette, "Archetypes of American Innocence: Lydia Blood and Daisy Miller", *American Quarterly*, 5 (1953): 31-38.

Kirk, Clara M. and Rudolf Kirk, "Abraham Cahan and William Dean Howells: The Story of a Friendship", *American Jewish Historical Quarterly*, 52 (1962): 27-57.

----, "William Dean Howells, George William Curtis, and the Haymarket Affair", *American Literature*, 40 (January, 1969): 487-98.

Klinkowitz, Jerome F., "Ethic and Aesthetic: The Basil and Isabel March Stories of William Dean Howells", *Modern Fiction Studies*, 16 (1970): 303-22.

Lindberg-Seyersted, Brita, "Three Variations of the American Success Story: The Careers of Luke Larkin, Lemuel Barker and Lemuel Pitkin", *English Studies*, 53 (1972): 1-16.

Long, Robert E., "The Ambassadors and the Genteel Tradition: James Correction of Hawthorne and Howells", *New England Quarterly*, 42 (1969): 44-64.

Love, Glen A., "The Landlord at Lion's Head: Howells and The Riddle of the Painful Earth", *Old Northwest*, 10 (1984): 107-25.

Lydenberg, John and Edwin H. Cady, "The Howells Revival: Rounds Two and Three", *New England Quarterly*, 32 (1959): 394-407.

Maffi, Mario, "Architecture in the City, Architecture in the Novel: William Dean Howells' A Hazard of New Fortunes", *Studies in Literary Imagination*, 16, No. 2 (1983), 35-43.

Marowitz, Sanford E., "Howells and the Ghetto: The Mystery of Misery", *Modern Fiction Studies*, 16 (1970): 345-62.

Martin, Robert K., "Hercules in Knickerbockers: Class, Gender and Sexuality in The Landlord at Lion's Head", *American Literary Realism*, 20 (1988).

Mathews, James W., "Towards Naturalism: Three Late Novels of W.D. Howells", *Genre*, 6 (1973): 362-75.

McMurry, William, "The Concept of Complicity in Howells' Fiction", *New England Quarterly*, 35 (1962): 489-95.

Miler, Elsie, "The Feminization of American Realist Theory", *American Literary Theory*, 23 (1990): 20-41.

Murphy, Brenda, "American Realism and the Limits of Critical Theory", *Modern Language Studies*, 16 (1986): 81-88.

---, "Howells and the Popular Story Paradigm: Reading Silas Lapham's Proairetic Code", *American Literary Realism*, 1989 Winter, 21 (2): 21-33.

Nettels, Elsa, "Howells and Hardy", *Colby Library Quarterly*, 20 (1984): 107-22.

---, "Howells and Ibsen", *Texas Studies in Literature and Language*, 20 (1978): 153-68.

---, "One and Many: Howells' Treatment of Race", *American Literary Realism*, 18 (1985): 72-91.

Parrington, V.L., "William Dean Howells and the Realism of the Commonplace", *Main Currents in American Thought*, New York: Harcourt, 1930, III.

Parker, Gail Thain, "William Dean Howells: Realism and Feminism", *Uses of Literature*, ed. Monroe Engel., Cambridge: Harvard University Press, 1973: 133-61.

Parks, Edd Winifield, "A Realist Avoids Reality: W.D. Howells and the Civil War Years", *South Atlantic Quarterly*, 52 (1953): 93-97.

Pizer, Donald, "The Ethical Unity of The Rise of Silas Lapham", *American Literature*, 32 (1960): 322-27.

Perkins, George, "A Modern Instance: Howells' Transition to Artistic Maturity", *New England Quarterly*, 47 (1974): 427-39.

Perkins, George, "Howells and Hawthorne", *Nineteenth Century Fiction*, 15 (1960): 295-62.

Porte, Joel, "Manners, Morals and Mince Pie: Howells' America Revisited", *Prospects*, 10 (1985): 443-60.

Quinn, Arthur Hobson, "William Dean Howells and the Approach to Realism", *A History of the American Drama from the Civil War to the Present Day*, New York: Appleton, 1936, I.

—, "William Dean Howells and the Establishments of Realism", *American Fiction: an Historical and Critical Survey*, New York: Appleton, 1936.

Reeves, John K., "The Limited Realism of Howells' Their Wedding Journey", *PMLA*, 77 (1962): 617-28.

Reeves, John K., "The Way of a Realist: A Study of Howells' Use of the Saratoga Scene", *PMLA*, 65 (1950): 1035-42.

Rife, David, "Hamilton Wright Mabie and W.D. Howells: A Literary Friendship", *American Literary Realism*, 19 (1987): 30-40.

Rother, James, "Face-Values on the Cutting-Room: Some Versions of the Newer Realism", *American Literary Realism*, 21 (1989): 67-96.

Scharnhorst, Gary F., "Maurice Thompson's Regional Critique of William Dean Howells", *American Literary Realism*, 9 (1976): 57-63.

Schneider, Robert W., "William Dean Howells: The Nugwump Rebellion", *Five Novelists of the Progressive Era*, New York: Columbia University Press, 1965.

See, Fred D., "The Demystification of Style: Metaphoric and Metonmymic Language in A Modern Instance", *Nineteenth Century Fiction*, 28 (1974): 379-408.

See, Fred G., "Howells and the Failure of Desire", *Desire and the Sign: Nineteenth-Century American Fiction*, Baton Rouge: Louisiana State University Press, 1987.

—, "Howells and the Nature of Fathers", *American Literary Realism*, 20 (1988).

Seelye, John. "The Rise of William Dean Howells", *New Republic*, 165 (July 3, 1971): 23-26.

Sister Mary Petrus Sullivan, "The Function of Setting in Howells' The Landlord at Lion's Head", *American Literature*, 35 (1963): 38-52.

Sokoloff, B.A., "William Dean Howells and the Ohio Village: A Study in Environment and Art", *American Quarterly*, 11 (1959): 58-75.

Spangler, George M., "Moral Anxiety in A Modern Instance", *New England Quarterly*, 46 (1973): 236-49.

Storheff, Gary P., "Ironic Technique in The Landlord at Lion's Head", *North Dakota Quarterly*, 46, No. 2 1978): 55-64.

Solomon, Eric, "Howells, Houses, and Realism", *American Literary Realism*, 4 (1968): 89-93.

Solomon, Roger B., "Realism as Disinheritance: Twain, Howells and James", *American Quarterly*, 16 (1964): 531-44.

Stein, Allen F., "William Dean Howells", *After the Vows were Spoken: Marriage in American Literary Realism*, Columbus, Ohio State University Press, 1984.

Stronks, James, B., "A Modern Instance", *American Literary Realism*, 4 (1968): 75-103.

Stephens, Gary, "Haunted Americana: The Endurance of American Realism", *Partisan Review*, 44, (1977): 71-84.

Tanselle, G. Thomas, "The Architecture of The Rise of Silas Lapham", *American Literature*, 37 (1966): 430-57.

Toth, Susen Allen, "Character and Focus in The Landlord at Lion's Head", *Colby Library Quarterly*, 11 (1975): 116-28.

Ube, George R., "Status and Contact: The Divorce Dispute of the Eighties and Howells' A Modern Instance", *Colby Library Quarterly*, 19 (1983): 78-89.

Updike, John, "A Critic at Large: Howells as Anti-Novelist", *New Yorker*, 63, No. 1 (13 July, 1987): 78-88.

Vanderbilt, Kermit, "From Passion to Impasse: The Structure of a Dark Romantic Theme in Hawthorne, Howells and Barth", *Studies in the Novel*, 8 (1976): 419-29.

---, "Marcia Gaylord's Electra Complex: A Footnote to Sex in Howells", *American Literature*, 34 (1962): 365-74.

Vidal, Gore, "The Peculiar American Stamp", *New York: Review of Books*, 30 (27 (October 1983): 45-55.

Wagenknecht, Edward, "The American Mirror: William Dean Howells", *Cavalcade of the American Novel*, New York: Holt, 1952.

Wasserstrom, William, "Howells' Mansion and Thoreau's Cabin", *College English*, 27 (1965): 366-72.

Wasserstrom, William, "Howells' and the High Cost of Junk", *Old Northwest*, 10 (1984): 77-90.

---, "William Dean Howells: The Indelible Stain", *New England Quarterly*, 32 (1959): 486-95.

---, Wilson, Christopher P., "Markets and Fictions: Howells' Infernal Juggle", *American Literary Realism*, 20 (1988).

Wright, Ellen, F., "Given Bartley, Given Marcia: A Reconsideration of Howells' A Modern Instance", *Texas Studies in Literature and Language*, 23 (1981), 213-31.

Wright, Ellen, F., "William Dean Howells and the Irrational", *Nineteenth Century Fiction*, 38 (1983): 304-23.

Books on Literary Theory

Abel, Darrel, *Masterworks of American Realism: Twain, Howells, James*, New York: Barron's Educational Series, 1963.

Allot, Miriam, ed., *Novelists on Novel*, New York: Columbia University Press, 1959.

Alter, Robert, *Partial Magic: The Novel as a Self-Conscious Genre*, Berkley: University of California Press, 1975.

Becker, George Joseph, ed., *Documents of Modern Literary Realism*, Princeton: Princeton University Press, 1963.

—, *Realism in Modern Literature*, New York: Ungar, 1980.

Bernadete, Jane, ed., *American Realism: A Shape for Fiction*, New York: Putnam, 1972.

Berthoff, Warner, *The Ferment of Realism: American Literature 1884-1919*, New York: Free Press, 1965.

Booth, Wayne C., *The Rhetoric of Fiction*, Chicago: University of Chicago Press, 1961.

Cady, Edwin H., *The Light of Common Day: Realism in American Fiction*, Bloomington: Indiana University Press, 1971.

Chase, Richar, *The American Novel and its Tradition*, Ludhiana: Kalyani Publishers, 1973.

Current-Garcia, Eugene, Patrick, Walton, R., *Realism and Romanticism in Fiction: An Approach to Novel*, Chicago: Scott, 1962.

Grant, Damian, *Realism*, London: Methuen, 1970.

Graff, Gerald, *Literature Against Itself: Literary Ideas in Modern Society*, Chicago: University of Chicago Press, 1979.

Habegger, Alfred, *Gender, Fantasy and Realism in American Literature*, New York: Columbia University Press, 1982.

Hemmings, F.W.J., *The Age of Realism*, Sussex: The Harvester Press, 1978.

Hicks, Granville, *The Great Tradition: An Interpretation of American Literature Since the Civil War*, New York: Macmillan, 1933.

Hubell, Jay B., *Who are the Major American Writers?*, Durham: Duke University Press, 1972.

Kaplan, Amy, *The Social Construction of American Realism*, Chicago: University of Chicago Press, 1988.

Kazin, Alfred, *On Native Grounds: An Interpretation of Modern American Prose Literature*, New York: Harcourt, 1942.

Kerr, Howard, *Mediums and Spirit-Rappers and Roaring Radicals: Spiritualism in American Literature, 1850-1900*, Urbana: University of Illinois Press, 1972.

Knight, Gran C., *The Critical Period in American Literature*, Chapel Hill: University of North Carolina Press, 1951.

Kolb, Harold, H., Jr., *The Illusion of Life: American Realism as a Literary Form*, Charlottesville: University Press of Virginia, 1969.

Larkin, Maurice, *Man and Society in Nineteenth Century Realism Determinism in Literature*, London: Macmillan, 1980, 1977.

Lee, Brian, *American Fiction 1865-1945*, London: Longman, 1987.

Lewisohn, Ludwig, *Expression in America*, New York: Harper, 1932.

Lukacs, George, *Essays on Realism*, Cambridge: MIT Press, 1980.

—, *Studies in European Realism: A Sociological Survey of the Writings of Balzac, Stendhal, Zola, Tolstoy, Gorki and others*. Trans. Edith Bone, London: Hilway, 1950.

—, *The Meaning of Contemporary Realism*, Trans. John and Neeke Mander, London: Martin Press, 1963.

—, *The Historical Novel*, Trans. Hennah and Stanley Mitchell, London: Merlin Press, 1962.

Martin, Jay, *Harvests of Changes: American Literature 1865-1914*, Englewood Cliffs: Prentice Hall, 1967.

Mckay, Janet Holmgren, *Narration and Discourse in American Realistic Fiction*, Philadelphia: University of Pennsylvania Press, 1982.

Millgate, Michael, *American Social Fiction: James to Cozzen*, New York: Barnes, 1964.

Morgan, Howard Wayne, *American Writers in Rebellion from Mark Twain to Dreiser*, New York: Hill and Wang, 1965.

Mukherjee, Meenakshi, *Realism and Reality*, Delhi: Oxford University Press, 1965.

Murphy, Brenda, *American Realism and American Drama 1880-1940*, Cambridge: Cambridge University Press, 1987.

Pizer, Donald, *Realism and Naturalism in Nineteenth Century American Literature*, Carbondale: Southern Illinois University Press, 1984.

Spiller, Robert M., *The Cycle of American Literature*, New York: Macmillan, 1955.

Suchkov, Boris, *A History on Realism*, Moscow: Progress, 1973.

Stowe, William W., *Balzac, James and the Realistic Novel*, Princeton, N.J.: Princeton University Press, 1983.

Sundquist, Eric, J. Ed., *American Realism: New Essays*, Baltimore: John Hopkins University Press, 1982.

Tallis, Raymond, *In Defence of Realism*, London: Arnold, 1988.

Tuttleton, James W., *The Novel of Manners in America*, Chapel Hill: University of North Carolina Press, 1972.

Trachtenberg, Alan, *The Incorporation of America: Culture and Society in Gilded Age*, New York: Hill and Wang, 1982.

Van Doren, Carl, *The American Novel*, New York: Macmillan, 1921.

Vernon, John, *Money and Fiction: Literary Realism in the Nineteenth Century and Early Twentieth Centuries*, Ithaca: Cornell University Press, 1984.

Wann, Louis Ed., *The Rise of Realism: American Literature from 1860 to 1900*, New York: Macmillan, 1961.

Williams, D.A. ed., *The Monster in the Mirror: Studies in Nineteenth Century Realism*, Oxford: Oxford University Press, 1978.

Ziff, Larzer, *The American 1890s: Life and Times of a Lost Generation*, Chatto and Windus: London, 1967.

Index